EARLY CHILDHOOD ED

Sharon Ryan,

MW01005263

Inclusion in the Early Childhood Classroom:
What Makes a Difference?
SUSAN L. RECCHIA AND YOON-JOO LEE

Language Building Blocks:
Essential Linguistics for Early Childhood Educators
ANITA PANDEY

Understanding the Language Development and Early Education
of Hispanic Children.
EUGENE E. GARCÍA & ERMINDA H. GARCÍA

Moral Classrooms, Moral Children: Creating a Constructivist
Atmosphere in Early Education, 2nd Ed.
RHETA DEVRIES & BETTY ZAN

Defending Childhood:
Keeping the Promise of Early Education
BEVERLY FALK, ED.

Don't Leave the Story in the Book: Using Literature to Guide
Inquiry in Early Childhood Classrooms
MARY HYNES-BERRY

Starting with Their Strengths: Using the Project Approach in
Early Childhood Special Education
DEBORAH C. LICKEY & DENISE J. POWERS

The Play's the Thing:
Teachers' Roles in Children's Play, 2nd Ed.
ELIZABETH JONES & GRETCHEN REYNOLDS

Twelve Best Practices for Early Childhood Education: Integrating
Reggio and Other Inspired Approaches
ANN LEWIN-BENHAM

Big Science for Growing Minds:
Constructivist Classrooms for Young Thinkers
JACQUELINE GRENNON BROOKS

What If All the Kids Are White? Anti-Bias Multicultural Education
with Young Children and Families, 2nd Ed.
LOUISE DERMAN-SPARKS & PATRICIA G. RAMSEY

Seen and Heard:
Children's Rights in Early Childhood Education
ELLEN LYNN HALL & JENNIFER KOFKIN RUDKIN

Young Investigators: The Project Approach in the
Early Years, 2nd Ed.
JUDY HARRIS HELM & LILIAN G. KATZ

Supporting Boys' Learning: Strategies for Teacher Practice,
PreK–Grade 3
BARBARA SPRUNG, MERLE FROSCHL, & NANCY GROPPER

Young English Language Learners: Current Research and
Emerging Directions for Practice and Policy
EUGENE E. GARCÍA & ELLEN C. FREDE, EDS.

Connecting Emergent Curriculum and Standards in the Early
Childhood Classroom: Strengthening Content and Teacher
Practice
SYDNEY L. SCHWARTZ & SHERRY M. COPELAND

Infants and Toddlers at Work: Using Reggio-Inspired Materials
to Support Brain Development
ANN LEWIN-BENHAM

The View from the Little Chair in the Corner: Improving Teacher
Practice and Early Childhood Learning
(Wisdom from an Experienced Classroom Observer)
CINDY RZASA BESS

Culture and Child Development in Early Childhood Programs:
Practices for Quality Education and Care
CAROLLEE HOWES

The Early Intervention Guidebook for Families and Professionals:
Partnering for Success
BONNIE KEILTY

The Story in the Picture:
Inquiry and Artmaking with Young Children
CHRISTINE MULCAHEY

Educating and Caring for Very Young Children:
The Infant/Toddler Curriculum, 2nd Ed.
DORIS BERGEN, REBECCA REID, & LOUIS TORELLI

Beginning School: U.S. Policies in International Perspective
RICHARD M. CLIFFORD & GISELE M. CRAWFORD, EDS.

Emergent Curriculum in the Primary Classroom: Interpreting the
Reggio Emilia Approach in Schools
CAROL ANNE WIEN, ED.

Enthusiastic and Engaged Learners: Approaches to Learning in
the Early Childhood Classroom
MARILOU HYSON

Powerful Children: Understanding How to Teach and Learn
Using the Reggio Approach
ANN LEWIN-BENHAM

The Early Care and Education Teaching Workforce at the
Fulcrum: An Agenda for Reform
SHARON LYNN KAGAN, KRISTIE KAUERZ, & KATE TARRANT

Windows on Learning:
Documenting Young Children's Work, 2nd Ed.
JUDY HARRIS HELM, SALLEE BENEKE, & KATHY STEINHEIMER

Ready or Not: Leadership Choices in Early Care and Education
STACIE G. GOFFIN & VALORA WASHINGTON

Supervision in Early Childhood Education:
A Developmental Perspective, 3rd Ed.
JOSEPH J. CARUSO WITH M. TEMPLE FAWCETT

Guiding Children's Behavior:
Developmental Discipline in the Classroom
EILEEN S. FLICKER & JANET ANDRON HOFFMAN

The War Play Dilemma: What Every Parent and Teacher Needs
to Know, 2nd Ed.
DIANE E. LEVIN & NANCY CARLSSON-PAIGE

Possible Schools: The Reggio Approach to Urban Education
ANN LEWIN-BENHAM

Everyday Goodbyes
NANCY BALABAN

Playing to Get Smart
ELIZABETH JONES & RENATTA M. COOPER

(continued)

Early Childhood Education Series titles, continued

How to Work with Standards in the Early
Childhood Classroom
CAROL SEEFELDT

In the Spirit of the Studio
LELLA GANDINI ET AL., EDS.

Understanding Assessment and Evaluation in Early Childhood
Education, 2nd Ed.
DOMINIC F. GULLO

Teaching and Learning in a Diverse World, 3rd Ed.
PATRICIA G. RAMSEY

The Emotional Development of Young Children, 2nd Ed.
MARILOU HYSON

Effective Partnering for School Change
JIE-QI CHEN ET AL.

Let's Be Friends
KRISTEN MARY KEMPLE

Young Children Continue to Reinvent Arithmetic—
2nd Grade, 2nd Ed.
CONSTANCE KAMII

Major Trends and Issues in Early Childhood Education:
Challenges, Controversies, and Insights, 2nd Ed.
JOAN PACKER ISENBERG & MARY RENCK JALONGO, EDS.

The Power of Projects: Meeting Contemporary Challenges in
Early Childhood Classrooms—
Strategies and Solutions
JUDY HARRIS HELM & SALLEE BENEKE, EDS.

Bringing Learning to Life
LOUISE BOYD CADWELL

The Colors of Learning
ROSEMARY ALTHOUSE, MARGARET H. JOHNSON, &
SHARON T. MITCHELL

A Matter of Trust
CAROLLEE HOWES & SHARON RITCHIE

Widening the Circle
SAMUEL L. ODOM, ED.

Children with Special Needs
MARJORIE J. KOSTELNIK ET AL.

Developing Constructivist Early Childhood Curriculum
RHETA DEVRIES ET AL.

Outdoor Play
JANE PERRY

Embracing Identities in Early Childhood Education
SUSAN GRIESHABER & GAILE S. CANNELLA, EDS.

Bambini: The Italian Approach to Infant/Toddler Care
LELLA GANDINI & CAROLYN POPE EDWARDS, EDS.

Serious Players in the Primary Classroom, 2nd Ed.
SELMA WASSERMANN

Telling a Different Story
CATHERINE WILSON

Young Children Reinvent Arithmetic, 2nd Ed.
CONSTANCE KAMII

Managing Quality in Young Children's Programs
MARY L. CULKIN, ED.

The Early Childhood Curriculum, 3rd Ed.
CAROL SEEFELDT, ED.

Inside a Head Start Center
DEBORAH CEGLOWSKI

Bringing Reggio Emilia Home
LOUISE BOYD CADWELL

Master Players
GRETCHEN REYNOLDS & ELIZABETH JONES

Understanding Young Children's Behavior
JILLIAN RODD

Understanding Quantitative and Qualitative Research in Early
Childhood Education
WILLIAM L. GOODWIN & LAURA D. GOODWIN

Diversity in the Classroom, 2nd Ed.
FRANCES E. KENDALL

Developmentally Appropriate Practice in "Real Life"
CAROL ANNE WIEN

Experimenting with the World
HARRIET K. CUFFARO

Quality in Family Child Care and Relative Care
SUSAN KONTOS ET AL.

Using the Supportive Play Model
MARGARET K. SHERIDAN, GILBERT M. FOLEY,
& SARA H. RADLINSKI

The Full-Day Kindergarten, 2nd Ed.
DORIS PRONIN FROMBERG

Assessment Methods for Infants and Toddlers
DORIS BERGEN

Young Children Continue to Reinvent Arithmetic—3rd Grade:
Implications of Piaget's Theory
CONSTANCE KAMII WITH SALLY JONES LIVINGSTON

Diversity and Developmentally Appropriate Practices
BRUCE L. MALLORY & REBECCA S. NEW, EDS.

Changing Teaching, Changing Schools
FRANCES O'CONNELL RUST

Physical Knowledge in Preschool Education
CONSTANCE KAMII & RHETA DEVRIES

Ways of Assessing Children and Curriculum
CELIA GENISHI, ED.

Scenes from Day Care
ELIZABETH BALLIETT PLATT

Making Friends in School
PATRICIA G. RAMSEY

The Whole Language Kindergarten
SHIRLEY RAINES & ROBERT CANADY

Multiple Worlds of Child Writers
ANNE HAAS DYSON

The Good Preschool Teacher
WILLIAM AYERS

The Piaget Handbook for Teachers and Parents
ROSEMARY PETERSON & VICTORIA FELTON-COLLINS

Visions of Childhood
JOHN CLEVERLEY & D. C. PHILLIPS

Ideas Influencing Early Childhood Education
EVELYN WEBER

The Joy of Movement in Early Childhood
SANDRA R. CURTIS

Inclusion in the Early Childhood Classroom

What Makes a Difference?

SUSAN L. RECCHIA
YOON-JOO LEE

Teachers College, Columbia University
New York and London

Published by Teachers College Press, 1234 Amsterdam Avenue, New York, NY 10027

Library of Congress Cataloging-in-Publication Data

Recchia, Susan
    Inclusion in the early childhood classroom : what makes a difference
    Susan L. Recchia, Yoon-Joo Lee.
        pages cm. — (Early childhood education series)
    Includes bibliographical references and index.
    ISBN 978-0-8077-5400-9 (pbk.)
        1. Inclusive education—United States. 2. Early childhood education—
    United States. 3. Children with disabilities—Education (Early
    childhood)—United States. I. Title.
    LC1201.R44   2013
    371.9'0460973—dc23

                                                                2012035813

ISBN 978-0-8077-5400-9 (paper)

Printed on acid-free paper

Manufactured in the United States of America

20   19   18   17   16   15   14   13   8   7   6   5   4   3   2   1

This book is dedicated to young children and their teachers who are the heart of inclusion. Through their own unique stories and relationships, they inspire new possibilities for authentic and meaningful inclusive communities.

Contents

Acknowledgments   ix

**1. Introduction: Ways of Thinking About, Talking About,
and Taking Steps Toward Social Inclusion**   **1**

The Many Faces of Inclusion   1

The Need to Broaden the Research Framework   3

Traditional Ways of Looking at Inclusion   4

A Challenge to the Dominant Discourse About Inclusion   6

An Inclusive Learning Environment:

    Classroom Components and Teacher Competencies   8

Organization of the Book   10

**2. Welcoming Children with Disabilities to the Table:
Classroom Components That
Value Individual Differences**   **14**

What Researchers Say About the Social Competencies

    of Young Children with Special Needs   15

Positive Responses to Diverse Abilities   17

Mario's Story: Meeting the Needs of a Child with Cognitive Delays

    Who Is Motivated to Play with Others   18

Adam's Story: Meeting the Needs of a Child with Physical Disabilities

    Who Is Highly Motivated to Move Independently   23

Joey's Story: Meeting the Needs of a Child with Social Challenges

    Who Demonstrates Unusual Social Behaviors   28

Final Words: Bridging Developmental Differences   32

How Can You Make a Difference?

    Questions for Further Reflection   34

**3. Rethinking Social Inclusion: Classroom Components
That Empower All Children**   **36**

What Researchers Say About Social Inclusion of Children

    with Challenging Behaviors   36

Ira's Story: Dealing with a Child Who Is
    Marginalized in the Classroom   40
Cody's Story: Responding to an Aggressive Child   44
Abigail's Story: Attending to a Quiet Child Who
    Does Not Demand the Teachers' Attention   49
Final Words: Developing New Mind-sets to Promote
    Inclusive Classrooms That Value Everyone   55
How Can You Make a Difference?
Questions for Further Reflection   57

4. **Becoming a Teacher Who Makes a Difference:**
   Examining Values, Reconsidering Expectations,
   and Developing Competencies to
   Transform Classroom Practice   **59**
   Challenges of Inclusion   60
   What Researchers Say About the Role of Teachers in
       Facilitating Social Interactions in Early Childhood Classrooms 61
   A Reconceptualization of Early Childhood Inclusive Teaching   63
   The Six Teacher Competencies for an Inclusive Classroom   65
   Teacher Competencies as a Framework for Transforming Teaching
       and Learning in the Early Childhood Classroom   78

5. **Early Childhood Classrooms as Inclusive Learning**
   Communities: Our Visions for the Future   **82**
   Synthesizing the Components and Competencies
       Through a Relationship Lens   83
   The Overarching Principles for Inclusive Practice   84
   Bringing Early Childhood Inclusion to Life: Applying
       the Classroom Components and Teacher Competencies   87
   Where Do We Go from Here? Implications for
       Teacher Preparation and Professional Development   92

References   **95**

Index   **101**

About the Authors   **107**

Acknowledgments

B RINGING THIS BOOK to fruition was indeed a labor of love, inspired by children and teachers in many early childhood classrooms, and nurtured by friends, family, and supportive professionals. We offer our deepest gratitude to the children and teachers in the stories we have shared for their generosity in sharing their learning spaces and experiences with us. We thank the staff at Teachers College Press for helping to make our first book such a positive experience, and particularly Marie-Ellen Larcada, for her enthusiastic interest in our ideas and her constant encouragement. We are especially grateful to Sharon Ryan for her helpful feedback on our first drafts of several chapters. Our families, friends, and colleagues have been a constant source of support throughout the process, and we also extend to them our heartfelt thanks.

CHAPTER 1

Introduction

Ways of Thinking About, Talking About, and Taking Steps Toward Social Inclusion

W HAT DOES IT mean to be part of an early childhood classroom community? How do individual children experience a sense of community and relationships within their classrooms? How do their peers respond to and include them in everyday classroom activities? What do teachers do to facilitate social community? What can teachers do differently? How can teachers draw on ideas about what is taught in the ideal classroom and incorporate them into their real classrooms? What makes a classroom "inclusive"? Questions like these become quite compelling as classrooms and schools serve increasingly more diverse children and families. These kinds of questions also demand that we think holistically about teaching and learning within diverse early childhood classroom communities.

THE MANY FACES OF INCLUSION

Conceptualizations of inclusion often vary from site to site and the nature of the policies and philosophies that guide practice at each site reflect diverse interpretations of the construct of inclusive education. In this book we have chosen to present a range of classrooms serving young children so that all kinds of teachers might be able to see themselves in our stories. Principles of inclusion can be applied within a general education classroom serving just one child with special needs, an integrated classroom serving groups of children with and without disabilities, or even within a self-contained classroom where all of the children are labeled as "disabled." In our experience as both preschool teachers and teacher educators, we have found that inclusion and exclusion can happen for a wide variety of children in all kinds of set-

1

tings. Although we know that children's early experiences as members of classroom communities serve as the foundation on which lifelong patterns of social behavior are constructed (DEC/NAEYC, 2009), far too often the guidelines for meeting their diverse educational needs are considered apart from their broader social needs.

As we present images of different classrooms in the chapters of this book, we focus on challenges and process, not on the presentation of solutions and end products. Our book offers opportunities to imagine alternative ideas for building classroom communities and for taking steps to change practice.

This book is different from many other books addressing inclusion in several ways. First, we focus on differences in children's abilities from a perspective of diversity as the norm (Baglieri & Knopf, 2004). Our purpose is not to articulate the deficits of particular children with disabilities in inclusive settings, but rather to see each child as a contributing member of the classroom community. While other books have categorized children by specific disabilities in ways that can make the problem of "fitting in" one that is based in children themselves, we attempt to shift the focus to a view of the classroom as a setting in which powerful group dynamics unfold, creating experiences of inclusion or exclusion for particular children.

One of our goals for this book is to provide a foundation for expanded discussions on the broader issue of building social community in early childhood classrooms. Today's early childhood settings are highly diverse, and serve a broad range of young children crossing many boundary lines (Odom, Vitztum, et al., 2004). Although our particular focus is on young children with identified special needs, we believe that the ideas presented here can be applied widely to address many forms of diversity. We include in our examples from practice a broad range of diverse settings and children, representing the many types of classroom settings that include children with special needs. We also present in our stories from the field real children with a variety of developmental delays and disabilities. We hope that by using broad strokes to paint this picture of the many possible ways to enact social inclusion, our ideas will have meaningful applications for a broad and diverse audience.

Having been classroom teachers ourselves, we understand the challenges involved in enacting responsive, high-quality teaching. Our goal is to help teachers look beyond the constraints of everyday practice to envision new possibilities. This book is not simply a set of classroom stories, as we also step back to look at things through a researcher's lens in our writing. While our focus is on classroom practices, we understand that all practice is embedded in philosophical beliefs that evolve from cultural assumptions, theoretical knowledge, and previous experiences (Valle & Connor, 2011). We hope that the structure of the book will invite preservice and in-service teachers to examine issues in their everyday practice which will raise larger questions about the global and far-reaching value in building truly inclusive classroom communities.

As we move into the 21st century, many more young children are being educated in settings described as "inclusive" (U.S. Department of Education, 2004). *Inclusion* has come to mean different things to different people, but for the purposes of this book we use the term primarily to describe early childhood settings where diverse groups of children have equal access to activities, curriculum, and social opportunities. The children and teachers that you will come to know in this book are located within a wide variety of early childhood classrooms. Some serve only children with disability labels, while others bring children with and without disability labels together. What gives these and other settings the potential for being inclusive goes far beyond the notion of which children are placed where.

THE NEED TO BROADEN THE RESEARCH FRAMEWORK

Although many scholars in the fields of child development and early childhood special education recognize the multidimensional nature of social experiences in early childhood special education classrooms (Kliewer, 2008), most research studies fail to focus on the broader contexts within which teacher-child and peer relationships develop. Recommended practices drawn from these "evidence-based" findings thus reinforce decontextualized ways of looking at social experiences without providing clear descriptions of the dynamic processes involved in building social relationships (Berry, 2006). These compartmentalized ways of examining children's and teachers' social behavior do not adequately account for the power of teacher and peer responses, both positive and negative, as a socializing influence. Taking a more holistic perspective, discussions of social experiences can extend to building early childhood classroom communities where teachers regard all children, and children regard each other, with respect, interest, and trust. Teachers' roles in this process extend beyond setting up activities and facilitating peer interactions and include how they relate to individual children on an interpersonal level (Erwin & Guintini, 2000). What teachers believe about students with disabilities is directly translated into what they teach. As Valle and Connor (2011) explain,

> A student with disabilities remains constant. What shifts is the concep-tualization of that student, depending upon who is doing "the looking." And how a teacher conceptualizes a student with disabilities has every-thing to do with the educational outcome for that student. (p. 13)

Having these intentions in mind, in the following chapters we describe how teachers can change their thinking—which can change their actions. We hope to inspire teachers to make true inclusion a reality within their everyday practice. Our conceptual framework, which focuses on classroom components and teacher competencies, has evolved over time and in response to our growing dissatisfaction with the limitations of dichotomous thinking about including chil-dren with disabilities. The brief overview below on the continuum from traditional, behavior-oriented ways of thinking about disability to more recent, philosophically oriented ways of thinking about inclu-sion is provided as a framework for understanding the broad body of knowledge that informs our eclectic approach to inclusion.

TRADITIONAL WAYS OF LOOKING AT INCLUSION

Inclusion is one of the most popular topics discussed in the field of special education. A review of the literature in this area uncovers many guidebooks (e.g., Guralnick, 2001; Kostelnik, Onaga, Rohde, & Whiren, 2001) that profess best practices and particular teaching strategies geared toward favorable outcomes, without really examin-ing the question of how early childhood teachers learn the process of facilitating social community in their classrooms. Typically, the effectiveness of inclusion has been evaluated through measuring spe-cific outcomes for children with disabilities (Purcell, Horn, & Palmer, 2007). Large-scale studies on inclusion classrooms have documented beneficial impacts for children both with and without disabilities, resulting in positive gains such as increased and more meaningful social interaction (Guralnick, 2001).

Many researchers have examined the social competencies of pre-schoolers with special needs (Guralnick, 2006; Guralnick, Connor, & Johnson, 2011; Guralnick, Neville, Hammond, & Connor, 2007; Kopp, Baker, & Brown, 1992), and the ways in which they relate to peers with and without disabilities (Buysse, Goldman, & Skinner, 2002; Hestenes

& Carroll, 2000; Odom, Vitztum, et al., 2004). However, much of this work has focused narrowly on specific skills and behaviors, without examining the broader classroom context within which social interactions take place. Children's social interactions are categorized into particular variables, such as social initiation (a child's behavior seeking attention from peers), social interactions (duration), peer group size (1:1, small group, large group), play format (adult-directed vs. child-directed), and adult engagement (active vs. passive) (e.g., Boyd, Conroy, Asmus, McKenney, & Mancil, 2008). These variables are coded systematically by categories that describe, for example, the ways that a child seeks attention, leads in peer activities, imitates a peer, verbally communicates with a peer, or shows emotions to peers (Guralnick, Hammond, & Connor, 2006).

Outcomes of these behaviors are judged as either successful or unsuccessful according to the specific criteria and the peers' response to the child with disabilities. Along with individual social behaviors, the context of social interactions are examined by looking at categories of play (such as social play, parallel play, onlooker play, solitary play, and teacher interaction) and types of play activities (e.g., games with rules, dramatic play, constructive play, gross-motor play, and functional play) (Guralnick, Hammond, & Connor, 2006; Gularnick, Connor, & Johnson, 2011; Walker & Berthelsen, 2008). Social interactions are broken down into different components and analyzed quantitatively without taking into consideration underlying and subtle social nuances. For example, Boyd et al. (2008), define and count children's social interactions, then transform them into numerical constructs such as the percentage of positive social interactions. Conclusions about children's social behavior are then drawn based on these decontextualized calculations. In most studies like these, which are valued in the field as "evidence-based," little attention is given to evaluating how meaningful the social experience is to the child. As a result, these types of findings provide little information about how young children develop authentic social relationships with others in their classrooms.

Beyond social interactions, the literature also analyzes long-term peer relationships and friendships without situating them within a broader social context. Studies consider the following concepts: typologies of children's social acceptance (e.g., popular, neglected, rejected, controversial, average), various types of friendships and social relationships (e.g., acquaintances, unilateral relationships, just friends, good friends, best friends), levels of social structure (e.g., social interactions, mutual friendships, peer networks, or cliques), and the functions that children's friendships serve (e.g., companionship, intimacy and affection, emotional support, social comparison) (Buysse et al., 2002; Estell, Jones, Pearl, & Van Acker, 2009; Guralnick, 2010).

Together, these studies have examined social interactions and friendships using a comprehensive list of social behaviors and constructs based on "normative" social development. Comparing children with disabilities to their typically developing peers in this way has resulted in providing for the field a picture of the behavior patterns of children with disabilities that is defined only in terms of established social norms. Although this information has been considered valuable to understanding developmental differences in children with disabilities, the underlying assumptions regarding what "counts" as meaningful social behavior do not emerge from the children themselves. The resulting deficit-focused way of thinking about young children's capacities often overlooks the strengths they may bring to a classroom environment as active members of the community. When competence is defined within the construct of a normative developmental framework, there is little room for developmental diversity among children (Kliewer, 2006; Kliewer & Biklen, 2007). This way of talking and thinking about including children with disabilities in the early childhood classroom can lead to marginalization and exclusion, as children who see and respond to things in nonnormative ways are pigeon-holed as different, difficult, or deviant (Danforth & Gabel, 2006; Valle & Connor, 2011).

A CHALLENGE TO THE DOMINANT DISCOURSE
ABOUT INCLUSION

As a counterbalance to deficit-based understandings of disability and quantitative ways of measuring the experiences of children with disabilities, Disability Studies in Education (DSE) has emerged as a different framework for understanding disability. The philosophical orientation of DSE views disabilities as differences rather than deficits, and challenges traditional special education research by pointing out its hyperfocus on concepts of individual deficit (Danforth, 2006). Research on inclusion anchored in DSE examines issues of inclusion through the lens of its philosophical and ideological underpinnings, in contrast to traditional special education research, which focuses on measurable outcomes. A truly inclusive environment is established only when a broad range of abilities is accepted as natural and necessary to create a rich tapestry of diversity (Erwin & Guintini, 2000).

In the field of early childhood special education, Kliewer and his colleagues (Kliewer, 2008; Kliewer & Biklen, 2007; Kliewer et al., 2004) have applied the philosophy of DSE within the context of literacy activities for young children with diverse learning needs. Kliewer's work is framed around "the paradigm of full participation for all citizens in inclusive early childhood classrooms" (Kliewer, 2006, p. 101). The concept of "local understanding" (Kliewer & Biklen, 2007) is used to explain how children's disabilities need to be understood through the collective, interpretive, and imaginative dialogue of a particular community, apart from the abstract, often dehumanizing, and segregationist process of classifying disabilities. In one example, Kliewer and Biklen (2007) described how Nicolas, a boy with severe developmental delays, was constructed as a literate child but in need of different kinds of support than his classmates tended to require. For example, Nicholas's distracted behavior, such as not sitting with the group during story time, was interpreted differently by his teacher, as she explained to other children that "he is listening to the book from the kitchen [area of the classroom]. That's where he listens best right now." Kliewer and Biklen (2007) elaborated on this situation this way:

> In Nicholas's classroom, the collaborative, democratic nature of the dialogic occurred on two levels. First, multiple voices belonging to adults who had direct, immediate, and deep roles in Nicholas's daily life converged to better understand and imagine Nicholas's literate participation in the classroom. Second, Nicholas's own communication contributed to the dialogic. While his actual voice may have been difficult to understand, his behaviors were read and interpreted from the perspective of supporting his participation in valued activities. Thus his resistance to joining the group was not interpreted as Nicholas not belonging; rather, his behavior meant only that joining the group required new ways of imagining how Nicholas would be supported as a full citizen of his classroom community. (p. 2589)

This body of research reflects a personal and communal commitment to struggle, advocacy, political and cultural change, and democratic participation in the daily experience of individuals labeled disabled (Kliewer, 2006). We embrace the underlying principles of DSE, and view children with special needs through a strengths-based perspective of diversity as the norm (Danforth, 2006; Valle & Connor, 2011). In this book, we will take the extra step of articulating concrete ways that each child can be a contributing and valued member in an inclusive classroom community. Inclusion is conceptualized as more than a placement, a set of strategies, or the abstract ideas associated with terms such as social justice and educational equity. We believe that true inclusion can only become a reality when a state of mind is translated into action within everyday classroom practice.

AN INCLUSIVE LEARNING ENVIRONMENT: CLASSROOM COMPONENTS AND TEACHER COMPETENCIES

Using the stories of children and teachers in real classrooms as a framework, we explore a set of complex ideas behind the construct of difference and inclusion in early childhood settings. We will address a wide array of issues that contribute to our understanding of what makes a difference, including the role of development, ways of honoring different learning styles, building a sense of classroom community, addressing power dynamics in the classroom, and responding to conflict with both teachers and peers.

Our vision of inclusive early childhood classrooms is framed by a set of classroom components and teacher competencies, which will guide the unfolding of our ideas throughout the book. We begin by presenting multiple stories of children and their teachers in inclusive early childhood classrooms, describing those elements that most contribute to building community and social inclusion, and raising questions about what more can be done or what can be done differently. Our goal in these chapters is to encourage readers to think more deeply about possibilities for change in their own classroom practice.

We have identified six classroom components that we believe are essential elements in building a socially inclusive early childhood classroom. They focus on overarching principles related to the social and physical classroom environment.

- There are multiple ways to be engaged in teaching and learning, and multiple ways to demonstrate knowledge and understanding.
- Opportunities for interpersonal connections and social support for all members of the community are built into the structure of the day.
- The environment is designed in a way that takes difference into consideration.
- Children's individual differences are integrated as value-added components of the curriculum, rather than viewed as interferences or hindrances.
- All kinds of students are accepted and respected as important and integral members of the classroom community.
- Support is provided for young children with a wide array of skills, abilities, strengths, and needs, to help them reach their full potential.

In order to put this vision into practice, we believe that teachers need to develop the following six competencies. We focus here on teachers' values and dispositions that play a critical role in bringing inclusion to life in their classrooms.

- Ways of thinking/ways of being that embrace difference and capitalize on opportunities to bring children together
- The capacity to nurture and embrace each child as a unique individual who brings a special contribution to the group
- Openness to reconsidering, rethinking, and redoing teaching and learning activities with children in response to their input
- The ability to attend to the child's perspective when making decisions that impact daily experiences
- The expectation that all children can meet appropriate educational and developmental goals and a willingness to support their efforts; a belief that children can and will be successful
- An understanding that "equity" does not always mean "equality" in an inclusive environment; because different people need different things to have "equal" access, treating children differently is acceptable

Although our stories highlight individual children and teachers, our focus is on classrooms as communities that embrace diverse learners. We look across multiple contexts and diversities to focus on the following themes: challenges and opportunities presented by diverse learners in a wide range of early childhood classrooms; what teachers can do to help build supportive physical and interpersonal environments in their classrooms for all kinds of children; and ways to reconceptualize teaching and learning as truly inclusive practices. Thus this book puts a strong emphasis on how teachers can change their thinking, which can change their actions and ways of being.

Our subtitle, *"What Makes a Difference?"* asks multiple questions. First, what makes us see a child as "different"? What are the parameters within which we define or describe learning differences in young children? How, and why, do we determine that a particular child has "special needs"? Second, what does it mean to be different? How are differences recognized and responded to in the group? What impact does being different have on others? Third, what can teachers do to make a difference? Compartmentalized and decontextualized ways of examining children's behavior don't adequately account for the power of others' responses, both positive and negative, as a socializing influence. How do teachers miss or provide opportunities to build on children's differences as strengths? And fourth, how do different kinds of social environments make a difference in promoting an inclusive classroom community where multiple learning styles can flourish?

ORGANIZATION OF THE BOOK

In this book we share stories from our own practice and research about several young children identified with different kinds of disabilities and their teachers, within different types of early childhood classrooms. We explore the ways that children's teachers and peers respond within natural classroom contexts, examining both those opportunities that are capitalized on as well as those that are missed. As shown in Table 1.1 at the end of this chapter, the book describes stories from a wide range of classrooms.[1] We purposefully selected the range of settings discussed in the chapters to illustrate that inclusion is a valued practice that can be enacted across placements. Thus we do not present one ideal classroom but draw on real ones where things go wrong each day and there are many missed opportunities. We hope that our presentation of real classrooms with real challenges and opportunities and children like those whom many teachers will meet at some point in their teaching careers will resonate with our readers.

Chapters 2 and 3 are focused on classroom components, using stories of individual children to discuss how children can be supported differently to build a more inclusive community. In Chapter 2, we present the stories of three children (Adam, Mario, and Joey) who approach the world in different ways due to their physical, cognitive, and social abilities. Chapter 3 includes a set of classroom stories of three other children (Ira, Cody, and Abigail) whose behaviors can be quite challenging for their classmates as well as their teachers. These two chapters follow the same format: They start with a brief introduction and review of literature on related topics. While research on inclusion of children with learning differences is discussed in Chapter 2, the literature presented in Chapter 3 addresses the ways that teachers are both thinking about and responding to challenging behavior in their classrooms.

After this brief survey of the literature, we provide a clear summary of what happened in each example (child/teacher/classroom story). We focus on one specific aspect of the story to connect theory and practice and provide alternative strategies that can help readers implement changes in their practice. Following these alternative strategies, we present a set of questions to encourage deeper thinking. Each story ends with a discussion on how one specific component is highlighted. Six stories address each of the six components listed earlier, and these six components are used as a frame for analyzing the classrooms and teaching practices presented, providing clearer descriptions of the ways that the components can be enacted.

Whereas Chapters 2 and 3 focus on the six classroom components, Chapter 4 addresses the six competencies that teachers need to develop to become more inclusive in their practice. The six teacher competencies are used as a framework to help readers think more deeply and specifically about the teacher's role in creating a truly inclusive classroom. We take you through the process of reflecting on both the real actions of the teachers presented in the previous chapters, as well as other possible ways of enacting inclusion in your own classrooms or potential classrooms. We see this chapter as the place to further articulate the processes that teachers need to engage in to become highly competent inclusion specialists. We discuss the critical role of reflection in examining your own biases and willingness to step outside of your comfort zones and we go back to the stories presented in previous chapters to bring more in-depth understanding to the teachers' practices.

In Chapter 5 we wrap up the ideas presented in the previous chapters, emphasizing what the reader will have learned from this book and how to begin to put the ideas into action. We also see this chapter as a place to make larger connections between our specific focus on the world of the day-to-day classroom and the overarching context surrounding it. Our primary goals for the book are also reiterated here: Through an illumination of what is possible, we hope to help teachers envision their own potential transformations in their practice and new possibilities for enacting social inclusion in a wide variety of classrooms.

NOTE

1. All names used throughout this book are pseudonyms.

TABLE 1.1. An Overview of Classroom, Teacher, and Child Characteristics

Child's Characteristics	Teacher's Characteristics	Classroom Context
Adam is a 4-year-old boy diagnosed with spina bifida and hydrocephalus. He is a happy, affectionate, and social child who is very determined to move independently despite his physical limitations.	*Jenny* is a special education teacher with 15 years of experience. She highly values meeting children's social needs in the early childhood classroom, and recognizes the value of independent movement to Adam.	This is a self-contained, preschool special education classroom located in a hospital rehabilitation center. All children have diagnosed disabilities, including physical and neurological impairments. They demonstrate a wide range of competencies across developmental domains.
Mario is a 2-year-old boy diagnosed with hypotonia, which causes motor and language delays. Very aware of others' activities, he follows them with interest. He uses vocalization and gestures as well as locomotion in his initiations and responses to both peers and adults.	*Aurelia* is a graduate student in Early Childhood Special Education, enrolled in a practicum course at the college where the child care program is based and has no extensive prior experience working in inclusive child care. Her philosophy is: "I always try to put myself in the child's shoes. If I am this child, what would be fun for me? Sometimes it does not work, but it's been useful in avoiding having conflicts with them."	This is a university-based, infant/toddler child care program that serves as a training site for graduate students. The program provides relationship-based care within an interage group for up to ten children aged 6 weeks to 36 months. The mixed-age group provides a natural context for daily adaptations to the curriculum.
Joey is a 4-year-old boy diagnosed with Pervasive Developmental Disorder Not Otherwise Specified (PDD NOS). He is a happy, playful child who sometimes experiences difficulties in relating and communicating with peers and adults in the classroom.	*Kathy* is a general education teacher with 1 year of experience. She feels her least effective strategy is "sticking to rote learning," but an important thing to be added to her curriculum to enhance students' progress would be "more books to stimulate new ideas and pictures for the children to learn from and share with each other."	This is a prekindergarten, integrated classroom in a large, urban, early childhood special education preschool. The school serves children with and without special needs; approximately half of the children have diagnosed disabilities.

12

TABLE 1.1. Continued.

Child's Characteristics	Teacher's Characteristics	Classroom Context
Ira is a 4-year-old boy with mild developmental delays (no specific diagnosis). He is socially aware and shows a preference for other boys. He tends to play with younger children and often needs the teacher's assistance when involved in complex play with peers his own age. He likes to listen to storybooks and engage in simple, repetitive activities.	*Beverly* and *Reah* both have several years of previous experience with preschoolers in an inclusion classroom. One prepared as an early childhood general educator and one as an early childhood general and special educator. They describe themselves as being "pretty fair," "funny," and "willing to respond to children's individual needs." They want to work on building an early childhood classroom community with an emphasis on social and emotional development.	This is a preschool classroom of a university-affiliated child care center. It serves a mixed-age group of 3- to 5-year-old children and follows an emergent curriculum philosophy, featuring a flexible and primarily child-centered, play-based curriculum.
Cody is a 3½-year-old boy, diagnosed with emotion regulation issues. He is a bright, physically active, and socially aware child who exudes energy in a way that often makes it hard to keep his hands to himself. He enjoys participating with the group in social activities, but at times his enthusiasm becomes overwhelming to himself and others.	*Camille* is an early childhood special educator with 3 years of experience. She demonstrates a very calm and centered presence in the classroom, and is good at explaining things to the children and preparing them for what will happen next.	This is an integrated preschool classroom for children between 3 and 5 years old. There are nine children enrolled in the class, five of whom are receiving special education services.
Abigail is a 3½-year-old girl diagnosed with a language delay. She is primarily an onlooker who attends to many activities, watching as others share ideas, and occasionally engaging in very brief verbal exchanges with adults and peers. During typical large-group activities, it is common for her to say nothing at all.	*Lorna* and *Mary* together have many years of classroom experience, one as a general educator for 15 years and the other as a special educator for 6 years. They focus on preparing students for success in kindergarten and rank language and social development at the top of their list of priorities.	This is an integrated prekindergarten classroom for children between 3½ and 5 years old. There are 16 children enrolled in the class, half of whom are receiving special education services.

CHAPTER 2

Welcoming Children with Disabilities to the Table

Classroom Components That Value Individual Differences

ARLY CHILDHOOD CLASSROOMS are by nature diverse places as young children come in so many shapes and sizes. In addition to their unique ways of being, infants and preschoolers are also in a unique stage of learning and greatly influenced by the environments that surround them. Their ability to make sense of the world is constantly in flux and can change rapidly and dramatically in the course of a year in a classroom. Because most preschool teachers are prepared to expect a range of behaviors and competencies among their students and most preschool children are quite comfortable adjusting to developmental differences in their peers, some see the preschool years as the most natural time for classroom inclusion (Guralnick, 2001; Mogharreban & Bruns, 2009).

Our observations, however, have revealed that beneath the surface of a diverse group of children interacting in one classroom lie curricular challenges that can defy the awareness of even teachers themselves. When particular children are distinctly different from the rest of their classmates in their learning styles, physical abilities, or social responsiveness, teachers often struggle to fully include them in the group. They must make adaptations in their classroom environments and in the ways they respond to children with developmental differences to support their full membership in the classroom community.

In this chapter we take an in-depth look at three of the classroom components that contribute to creating a socially inclusive early childhood classroom. We tell the stories of three children identified with particular special needs, paying close attention to their social experiences in their respective classrooms. We analyze what is happening, raise questions about possible changes that can be made, and suggest alternatives that we believe can make a difference for children, their peers, and their teachers.

WHAT RESEARCHERS SAY ABOUT THE SOCIAL COMPETENCIES OF YOUNG CHILDREN WITH SPECIAL NEEDS

The preschool years are considered a period of rapid growth in the development of peer relationships and friendships. The kinds of opportunities available to young children to learn about and experience relationships with their peers can significantly impact their understandings of both prosocial and antisocial behaviors and their formation of self-concepts (Brown, Odom, & McConnell, 2008; Guralnick, 2010; Walker & Berthelsen, 2008). Findings from traditional research in the fields of developmental psychology and special education have indicated that children's cognitive and language development are both reflected in and influence the ways that they interact with peers and form friendships.

Research on differences in social behaviors and interactions for young children with and without disabilities in inclusive classrooms indicates that children with disabilities engage in social interaction with peers less often than typically developing children (Odom, 2000). In many studies, Guralnick and his colleagues have also found that preschool children with disabilities are less successful in their social bids to peers, take the lead in interactions less often, and have more disruptive play when entering the play group than their "typical" peers (Guralnick, 2010; Guralnick, Connor, Hammond, Gottman, & Kinnish, 1996; Guralnick, Hammond, & Connor, 2006; Guralnick, Neville, et al., 2007; see also Kopp et al., 1992). Children with developmental delays may find it difficult to incorporate the tools needed to accomplish social tasks, such as entering a peer group or maintaining play within the free play environment (Guralnick, Hammond, & Connor, 2006). There is a close connection between varying levels of children's peer-related social competence and patterns of social isolation (Guralnick, 2006). When children with developmental delays have problems regulating their emotions in interpersonal relationships, it is difficult for them to form peer relationships, and this tends to lead to subsequent social isolation from peers.

Other studies have also shown that children with special needs don't always interact with peers in the same ways as typically developing children. They tend to spend more time in solitary play and onlooker behavior than their typically developing peers (Hestenes & Carroll, 2000; Kopp et al., 1992). They are considered more likely to be intrusive and disruptive during peer-group entry attempts than comparable groups of typically developing children, and use fewer emotion regulation strategies (Kopp et al., 1992). They are also more likely to remain in teacher-directed activities, and teachers engage in interaction with them more often than do peers (Brown & Bergen, 2002). Young children with disabilities are said to display infrequent interactions with peers regardless of the characteristics of class activities, while typical children respond positively to activities expected to promote peer interaction (Hamilton, 2005).

Several studies have taken a close look into other factors, such as different settings and different types of disabilities, that can affect differences in behavior in social relationships and friendship formation. For example, Buysse et al. (2002) found that the severity of a child's disability is not related to the number of reported friends, but a subsequent analysis suggested that children with disabilities enrolled in child care are 1.73 times more likely to have at least one friend than are their counterparts in specialized classes, even after controlling for severity of disability. This study implied that inclusion settings provide more social benefits for children with disabilities. While Buysse et al. (2002) discussed the impact of settings, Odom, Zercher, and Li (2006) found that socially accepted children tend to have disabilities that are less likely to affect social problem solving and emotional regulation, whereas children who were socially rejected had disabilities that were more likely to affect such skills and developmental capacities.

Many recent studies on social relationships with peers have focused on children who are diagnosed with autism, in part due to a sharp increase in children with this diagnosis over the past decade. Boyd et al. (2008) found that small groups, including 1:1 peer to target-child ratios, child-directed activities, and limited adult engagement, increase the likelihood of social initiations and social interactions between children with Autism Spectrum Disorder (ASD) and their same-age peers. These children have been shown to make gains in language, social skills, cognition, engagement in routines, and reductions in ASD symptoms in inclusive settings (Strain & Bovey, 2011). Even though this study was done with a specific population, this pattern of social behavior has also been observed with children with other developmental delays, as discussed above.

POSITIVE RESPONSES TO DIVERSE ABILITIES

Below we tell the stories of three children—Mario, Adam, and Joey—who approach the world in different ways due to their cognitive, physical, and social abilities (refer to Table 1.1 for further background information). The stories of these children verify some of the research points described above. Some of their social behaviors seem different from what we have learned is "typical" for most young children. Our goal is to reframe the more traditional deficit-oriented, linear approach to understanding children's interactions and, in each case, explore the ways that teachers can successfully maximize children's opportunities to be contributors to and members of the group.

Three classroom components are used as a framework for describing the children's stories:

Component 1. *There are multiple ways to be engaged in teaching and learning, and multiple ways to demonstrate knowledge and understanding.*

Traditionally, special educators have been prepared to teach children with special needs by focusing on skills and knowledge that will allow them to "catch up" with their typically developing peers. This way of teaching does not always allow teachers to observe and capitalize on how children with disabilities or developmental delays respond to activities and make meaning in their own ways and at their own levels. We are not arguing that the teacher needs to "dumb down" the cognitive level of the activity to include children with disabilities. Rather, to create more inclusive experiences, teachers need to create opportunities for peers to see that children with special needs can also participate as competent learners. When the activity is always centered on higher level skills, this is more likely to lead to situations that are highlighting what those with developmental delays can't do. When there are multiple ways to demonstrate knowledge and understanding, all the children, regardless of their functioning levels, can be valued participants, and what they bring to the table can be appreciated. When this happens, it is evidence of true inclusive experience.

Component 2. *Opportunities for interpersonal connections and social support for all members of the community are built into the structure of the day.*

To foster inclusive experience for all children, teachers need to consider the ways their classroom structures support everyone in the group. Sometimes the physical environment, routines, and daily classroom activities can actually interfere with, rather than provide a venue for, enhancing children's competencies. For example, because physical mobility can play such a significant part in social relationships, it is critical that teachers ensure that children with physical disabilities are not inadvertently left out of social experiences. Children's physical movement should be an important early childhood curriculum goal and a big part of their classroom experience. Even when it goes against the teacher's agenda and slows down the general flow of the classroom, all children's needs for moving independently must be acknowledged and honored. A missed opportunity occurs when a teacher fails to integrate the experience of a child who does not move as quickly as his peers into a broader social context so that other children recognize and understand his experiences.

Component 3. *The environment is designed in a way that takes difference into consideration.*

Individual differences are honored in multiple ways. The important message that this component shares is that children don't have to "give up" their idiosyncratic interests or desires; what is important to them can be incorporated in ways that embrace the needs and welfare of the group as a whole. For example, children who are diagnosed with autism or have other social-emotional issues may have different ways of interacting with others and may deal with social situations in unique ways compared with other children. This component emphasizes the importance of how children's diverse ways of engaging in the environment are acknowledged in the classroom and integrated through social connections between teachers and children as well as among children. Honoring differences in this way can establish a sense of community in a classroom, creating a more meaningful inclusive experience.

MARIO'S STORY:
MEETING THE NEEDS OF A CHILD WITH COGNITIVE
DELAYS WHO IS MOTIVATED TO PLAY WITH OTHERS

The first story illustrates Component 1: *There are multiple ways to be engaged in teaching and learning, and multiple ways to demonstrate knowledge and understanding.*

Mario is a very social boy with delays in cognitive and language development. Previous observations of young children with intellectual delays have revealed a lack of appropriate and effective social strategies, such as the ability to gain entry into playgroups or the ability to sustain a play sequence while interacting with peers (Guralnick, 2006). This story illustrates how developmental delays can impact the way a child enters and sustains play.

Inclusion Within a Mixed-Age Group

Mario attended an infant/toddler classroom at a university-based child care center with a mixed-age group of up to ten children aged 6 weeks to 36 months and a consistent adult-child ratio of at least one adult to three children. The mixed-age group provided a natural context for ongoing adaptations to the curriculum. This classroom provided daily routines but no fixed schedule in an attempt to accommodate infants' and toddlers' different needs regarding daily activities such as sleeping and eating. Because of the wide range of children's ages and abilities, this classroom was a place where a diverse set of children were accepted and respected as important and integral members of the classroom community. For example, the classroom materials and activities changed frequently in response to different children's needs, based on their developmental ages, growing interests, and changing abilities. A 6-week-old infant obviously needs different types of physical support than a 2-year-old toddler who is ready to actively explore his or her physical surroundings.

This program served as a professional preparation site for graduate students studying infant and toddler development and practice and provided relationship-based care within the context of an early education setting. Caregivers learned to observe and interpret children's cues and respond to their needs and requests on an individualized basis, while supporting their integration into the infant-toddler classroom. Each student caregiver was assigned a study infant or toddler as his or her "key child." As the "key caregivers" for these children, the students were expected to pay extra attention to them and to focus on them for their child observation assignments. However, the students were jointly responsible for all of the children at the center, and were not expected to have an exclusive one-to-one relationship with their key children. As a training site for graduate students, this program emphasized and enacted theory-practice connections.

Welcoming a Very Social Child to the Classroom

Mario was a 27-month-old toddler with special needs. Like many typically developing toddlers, he had his unique ways of participating in the social community of the classroom. He used vocalizations and gestures as well as locomotion in his initiations and responses to both peers and adults. After being cared for primarily by his mother at home, his first school experience as a toddler was in this inclusive classroom at the university-based infant and toddler child care program. Mario was diagnosed with hypotonia (a condition which caused his muscles to be relaxed in ways that slowed his motor development) and language delays. Reflections from the initial interview with his parents at the time of admission to the program illustrated how they saw his delays as obvious and significantly impacting his development. For example, his mother shared, "He is not doing many things that other kids his age are doing so I would like someone that is with him to help him with that, to stimulate him." His parents were especially concerned with his speech delay.

Although he showed some developmental delays in his social behavior, overall Mario was very aware of others' activities and often approached his peers with interest. For example, when he saw a child in the sandbox, he said "hi" to her, making a positive attempt to initiate an interaction. As shown in the following anecdote, he had a strong interest in younger children:

> Mario holds a wooden caterpillar by its string, dragging it on the floor. Behind him, a younger child crawls after the caterpillar. Mario slowly walks away from the child, holding tight to the caterpillar's string, looking at him, and saying "mine." The caregiver says to the younger child, "Sorry, Mario wants to play with it." The younger child continues to slowly crawl after him. The caregiver suggests that Mario give another toy to the child. She supports this by getting another toy and giving it to Mario to give to the baby. Mario picks up the toy, puts it in front of the baby, and talks to him.

Mario often stayed near a caregiver who was holding a baby, watching the baby very carefully. He sometimes responded to the negative behaviors of others directed toward him, but rarely initiated any conflict or negative interaction. Overall, he was a happy child who was very interested in other children.

The Importance of Careful Observation: Aurelia

Mario's key caregiver was Aurelia, a graduate student in Early Childhood Special Education, enrolled in a practicum course at the college at which the center was based. She didn't have extensive prior experience working with this age group or in inclusive child care. However, Aurelia seemed to be a very good observer of the children's behaviors and interactions and was very conscious of her own responses to them. In her journal she shared her philosophy: "I always try to put myself in the child's shoes. If I am this child, what would be fun for me? Sometimes it does not work, but it's been useful in avoiding having conflicts with them."

As she spent more time with Mario in the classroom, she grew in her understanding of his approach to sensory materials. Recording her observations in her journal, Aurelia wrote:

> He seems too careful about touching the paint (like not wanting to get his hands dirty). He does the same thing with play dough and goop. He loves watching it, loves watching other children manipulate the material, but he's reluctant to really handle the materials himself.

Aurelia worked hard to encourage and support meaningfully integrated social experiences. She often chose to work through peers to involve Mario when more competent peers were present. She incorporated higher levels of facilitation and explanation.

However, while Mario responded positively to teachers' interventions, he needed consistent cues to maintain interactions with peers, as shown in the following example.

> Mario is playing with Jane, a girl of his age, at the sandbox. The caregiver is also sitting next to them. The caregiver teaches Jane a game that compares the quantity of sand presented in two hands. When the caregiver puts out her two hands toward Mario, he just touches the sand in her hand, while Jane looks carefully at the caregiver's two hands to assess the quantity of sand they hold. Jane then holds sand in her hands and repeats several times, "Show me, show me which hand has the most." Then Jane turns to Mario and asks him several times, "Show me which hand has more." Mario just looks at her with a smile and explores the sand in the sandbox. The caregiver intervenes and asks Jane, "Can I choose?"

In this scene, Mario seemed unable to process his peer's attempts to involve him in a problem-solving game and focused on the simpler sensory task of exploring the sand. After repeated attempts to involve him in higher level play with no appropriate response, the peer reluctantly engaged the teacher in the game. This social interaction clearly reflected discrepancies in skills and abilities between these two children. Aurelia tried to build an opportunity for interpersonal connection between Jane and Mario. But because she didn't help Jane include Mario in a more meaningful way, in a sense she also didn't help Jane, the so-called more competent peer, to value what Mario could contribute to the interaction.

The Interaction Between Mario and Jane in the Sandbox

In this case the dilemma is, how can Mario be encouraged to interact meaningfully with same-age peers, like Jane, despite their cognitive differences around problem-solving activities? Aurelia seemed to have a preconceived notion that in order for Mario and Jane to be interacting around this activity, they must be able to somehow respond to it at the same level. Also the focus of what's happening in the sandbox shifted to what the more advanced peer, Jane, can do in the sand play when Aurelia responded to Jane by taking the role of competent peer. And Mario didn't seem to know what Jane was talking about. This led to a situation that, in a way, disenfranchised Mario. When Mario was not perceived as a peer who was likely to respond to Jane's mathematical question, the rules of the game were changed, focusing more on Jane's way of comparing different quantities instead of Mario's joy of exploring the sand.

The following excerpt from her journal shows Aurelia's honest confession regarding her struggle with being more drawn to a child with higher level thinking skills:

> I realize that although I am consciously trying to interact with Mario, when I'm with other kids it's so easy for me to ignore him or not to hear what he is saying, despite his very clear message . . . . How difficult it must be for children like Mario who are not heard as much as other children who make lots of noise.

Even though Aurelia makes a conscious effort to integrate Mario in interaction with his peers, it is challenging to foster opportunities for meaningful interpersonal connections among children functioning at different levels. There are several strategies to make this experience more inclusive, helping Jane value what Mario brings to the table.

Strategy 1: Jane can be encouraged and prompted to closely observe what Mario is doing. Aurelia could explain that Mario is not measuring the difference in the amounts of sand in her two hands but is more interested in exploring and feeling the sand. Aurelia can create an opportunity for Mario to explore the sand in his peer's hands, and emphasize the interesting texture and movement properties of the sand. Aurelia can do a little bit of both, so that the end result is to make Mario's presence more valuable.

Strategy 2: What Aurelia did in this situation was appropriate. She can still engage in the play at Jane's cognitive level and then follow up with an extension activity by pouring water into the sand, so that the play can become a sensory experience that can be enjoyed by both children.

Our recommended strategies in Mario's case are aimed at shifting the objective of the activity, so that the outcome/goal is something that he can do, is willing to engage in, and enjoys doing with a peer. When Mario's intent to enjoy the sensory experience of exploring sand is also highlighted, his peer, Jane, can be intrigued by his agenda and see him as a competent peer. If the teacher's goal is to bring children together and create a community, she needs to be able to enter an activity from a different place or perspective. She needs to observe and think about what the children can do together. That's where she can scaffold, focusing not just on higher level skills. In this case, the teacher can expand the sensory aspect of experience that both children can assimilate and enjoy together, as opposed to encouraging a level of engagement where one child will be automatically left out. Especially in an infant/toddler classroom, individual children develop at their own pace, and caregivers need to think about ways to stand back and create opportunities for children to value the contributions of peers who may demonstrate different competencies.

ADAM'S STORY: MEETING THE NEEDS OF A CHILD WITH PHYSICAL DISABILITIES WHO IS HIGHLY MOTIVATED TO MOVE INDEPENDENTLY

This story illustrates Component 2: *Opportunities for interpersonal connections and social support for all members of the community are built into the structure of the day.*

Children with physical limitations may face challenges when relating to peers. For example, their difficulty with physically approaching children for play can result in verbal compensations, such as shouting at children from a distance (Richardson, 2002). Also physical limitations can preclude participation in the activity, placing children as onlookers. The second story in this chapter is about Adam, a boy with physical disabilities who wants more than anything to move independently.

A Self-Contained Preschool Special Education Classroom

Adam attended a self-contained preschool special education classroom, located in a hospital rehabilitation center. Jenny was the head teacher in this class of 3- to 5-year-olds, where there were also two regular classroom assistants and other adults often present, such as therapists and nurses. All of the children had diagnosed disabilities, which included both physical and neurological impairments. They demonstrated a wide range of competencies across developmental domains. Some of the children were able to move freely about the classroom and engage in many physical activities, while others were more restricted in their movement. On any given day, attendance ranged from 6 to 10 children. (Because of the nature of these children's disabilities and their associated health issues, there was a high rate of absenteeism among the children.)

Unlike many early childhood special education self-contained classrooms which are more behaviorally oriented, this classroom provided a long period of semistructured free play each day, with many developmentally appropriate activities. The curriculum also included a range of preacademic activities that incorporated emergent reading and writing skills. This type of work was usually done in small groups, but occasionally the whole group was brought together for songs and special activities. For those children who needed adult assistance to engage with various aspects of the curriculum, this assistance was frequently provided. However, during extensive observation in this classroom, it was not unusual to see one or more children acting as onlookers as the more physically able children engaged in more complex play.

The adults worked hard to support each individual's learning differences, so that this classroom could be seen as "inclusive" in its own right. The children were able to engage with the curriculum in many different ways. Some had serious physical limitations that required a great deal of adult assistance, while others were able to navigate and communicate within the classroom quite independently.

Welcoming a Child Who Wants to Be Independent

Adam, a happy, affectionate, and social 4-year-old child, who was diagnosed with spina bifida and hydrocephalus, was very determined to move independently despite his physical limitations (he was able to move independently only by hitching himself along very slowly on his elbows while lying on the floor). He could use his arms and hands freely when his body was supported and was able to manipulate objects and engage in creative art activities alongside other children. Adam was very socially aware and fairly engaged in the classroom social dynamics. He had clear relationships with several of his peers with whom he played on a regular basis.

Adam had well-developed language skills and communicated easily with his peers using appropriate language. He asked for what he needed from teachers and usually let them know when he was uncomfortable. He anticipated favorite classroom activities and participated enthusiastically. Adam sometimes had clear and strong ideas about what he wanted to do and how he wanted to do it, and he was able to show great determination in following through with his goals.

Although there were other children in this classroom with physical limitations—some even more physically challenged than Adam—these children were not cognitively engaged in the way that he was. In order for Adam to engage with the other children in meaningful activities, however, somebody else had to manipulate his body. Thus at times he needed assistance to be a full participant in the play as he was unable to engage in many physical aspects of the activities on his own, as shown in the anecdote below. Here we see Adam as he chooses to push his own chair to the table for table-time activities.

> Jenny says, "You're pushing it." Adam says, "Right." He seems to have stopped moving. He's gone about 1 foot. The assistant teacher says, "Come on, Adam." She straddles him with her legs, so that she is standing over him, poised to help. Jenny asks, for the assistant's benefit it seems, "Your mommy said to push the chair?" Adam says, "Yeah, that's what my mommy says." He moves another few inches.

Once Adam got the chair close to the table, he needed assistance to get into it. Jenny continued to accommodate for Adam's assisted independence.

She holds the chair steady, asking, "Do you want it closer?" Adam says, "No." After a second, Jenny asks, "Are you close enough?" Adam says, "No." He is trying to climb into the chair but can't really do this on his own. Finally, Jenny says, "I'm going to help you—ready . . . 1 . . . 2 . . . 3." She lifts Adam into his chair. He had taken about 10 minutes to get there himself, across a distance of about 4 feet.

The Importance of Supporting Independence and Self-Esteem: Jenny

Adam's teacher, Jenny, recognized the value of this independent movement to Adam, and tried to encourage him to take the time he needed to scoot his body from place to place within the classroom. Jenny shared that she always tried to enhance her curriculum by being "more observant of when a child needs assistance and how much is truly necessary." An experienced teacher who highly valued meeting children's social needs in the early childhood classroom, Jenny felt that the least effective teaching strategy was "imposing too much structure in certain learning situations." Jenny appeared to know the children in her classroom, including Adam, very well. She understood Adam's particular dispositions, and made efforts to establish and maintain a positive social relationship with him. Jenny seemed to appreciate the ways that Adam brought his unique perspective to the classroom. She made individual adaptations in the ways she approached Adam; she involved him, whenever possible, in classroom activities; and she worked to successfully establish and maintain a special bond with him.

However, as shown in the anecdote below, allowing Adam to move independently frequently precluded his participation in activities with the other children because of the time involved.

Several children are playing in the block area while Adam is sitting by the table, located across the room. Adam sees them, and gets down from his chair and tries to move his body toward the block area. Jenny walks over to Adam, watching him move for a minute, and asks, "Adam, do you want me to carry you to the block area? I can take down some animals from the shelf and move them to the block area, so that you can build a zoo with Tommy and Johnny." Adam replies, "I'll move by myself. My mommy told me I could move by myself." With great determination, Adam continues to move his body inch by inch. While Adam is busy moving, Johnny and Tommy start building a zoo with blocks and animals. By the time Adam arrives at the block area, the other boys have finished with the zoo and moved to the library.

Jenny seemed unsure at times when to offer help and when to stand back. She wanted Adam to participate in group activities, but she also wanted to support his independent movement. How could she accomplish both of these goals?

The Interaction Between Jenny and Adam

The dilemma in this situation occurs when Adam wants to be independent, but Jenny wants to physically help him to make sure he can participate in a group activity. As shown in the anecdote above, she wanted to encourage him, and Adam wanted to show her that he could be independent. This was so important for him that he was willing to spend a half hour just to get across the very small room on his own. He was so proud of himself, and Jenny was proud of him too. But it was really hard for him to do this, and very exhausting. And Jenny was frustrated because she planned this small-group activity with him in mind, but it took such a long time for him to get to the block area that by the time he arrived, the other children had moved on to another activity.

In a case like this, many teachers start with the expectation that all children need to be participating in the same activities. But as an individual, Adam had another agenda that took precedence for him, namely, "I want to be able to get there by myself." He showed how he was determined to do that. In order for Adam to enact his agenda, however, the agenda set by the teacher (e.g., building a zoo in the block area with his two friends) had to be put on hold. Why is this so important for a truly inclusive classroom? Because it exemplifies the kind of flexible thinking that is required to make a difference. Allowing Adam to take his time to get around while still giving him opportunities to fully participate in the group requires adaptation. In situations like this, it is important to consider ways to change the physical environment and the nature of the activities, so that for children like Adam, physical mobility does not play such a significant part in social relationships. Instead of transitioning other children first and then bringing Adam to the activity area, different strategies can be used to make Adam's physical movement a part of his inclusive experience.

> *Strategy 1:* Other children can also engage in different ways to move their chairs to the table. They can move alongside Adam, so that while Adam is moving along, they can interact

with him. In this way, moving a chair with Adam is a natural part of the play experience.

Strategy 2: Teachers can create an activity in a confined space/area so that the physical transition to the activity can be somewhat less demanding. Rather than coming to the table which is far away on the other side of the room, Adam's required movement can be across a shorter distance, so that he can get there and access the activity independently.

Strategy 3: Teachers can come up with activities where everybody has to crawl. Crawling is something everybody does together, so that Adam can actually perform the task. Adam's way of crawling might be different from that of the other children, but everybody can have a similar experience. He can accomplish the same goal as somebody else, and this makes Adam's experience more inclusive and participatory. Additionally, teachers could set up obstacle courses in the room, and different children could go through them in different ways. Adam would most likely go through on his belly, creeping along, as that is his primary way of moving his body.

In this story, we see how important it is for Adam to move independently. His physical movement should be an important curriculum goal for him and a big part of his classroom experience. Jenny appreciates Adam's need for, and special interest in, moving independently. As we suggested above, Jenny can create an activity around movement with and for him. There are many ways to make movement experience a more integrated thread within the classroom, rather than just a separate activity for Adam that's not really connected to anything else.

JOEY'S STORY: MEETING THE NEEDS OF A CHILD WITH SOCIAL CHALLENGES WHO DEMONSTRATES UNUSUAL SOCIAL BEHAVIORS

This story illustrates Component 3: *The environment is designed in a way that takes difference into consideration.*

Teachers struggle to bring children into the group not only when they have physical and cognitive differences, but also when their social behaviors and responses are quite different from those of others. This is especially true for children with behavioral disabilities such as Pervasive Developmental Disorders (PDD) or one of the Autistic Spectrum Disorders (ASD). Increasing prevalence in rates of ASD have raised the likelihood that more children with this disability will be served in inclusive classrooms (Boyd et al., 2008). ASD is distinguished by social and communication difficulties. As a result, children with ASD tend to spend less time than their peers in activities requiring higher levels of social skills (Walker & Berthelsen, 2008) and make more social initiations during 1:1 or small groups in comparison to large-group activities (Boyd et al., 2008). The third story in this chapter is about a child with PDD and a teacher who uses different strategies to include him in her preschool classroom.

The Integrated Early Childhood Classroom: Bringing Together Diverse Learners Within an Inclusive Environment

Kathy's classroom was housed in a large, urban, early childhood special education preschool that served children from 2 through 5 years of age. Altogether there were 12 classrooms in the program, and Kathy's was one of two prekindergarten integrated classrooms that-served children with and without special needs inclusively, with approximately one-half of the children having diagnosed disabilities, primarily speech and language delays. There were 12 children in Kathy's room. All of the children were able to move around the classroom easily and to communicate with others, although they demonstrated a fairly wide range of skills and competencies.

Kathy worked with an assistant teacher, Doris, and they appeared to be great collaborators. They seemed to coordinate their efforts seamlessly, but on closer examination it was clear that they worked hard to stay in communication with each other throughout the day in subtle ways. Kathy and Doris spent time planning together before or after school, and frequently checked in with each other throughout the day using short verbal exchanges, facial expressions, and nonverbal communication such as nods and head shakes. They positioned themselves in the classroom so that each of them could be available to different small groups of children leading or scaffolding particular activities. There were frequently other adults present in the classroom, such as therapists or other observers, but Kathy's room maintained a playful atmosphere almost all the time.

The children were engaged in organized, semistructured free play periods throughout the day with many developmentally appropriate activities. Sometimes the morning included one or two more academically focused, planned activities such as a special story or a math game. Most of the time children worked in small groups at centers throughout the classroom, but each day included some whole-group activities such as "circle time," snack, and lunch.

Welcoming a Child with a Growing Sense of Self Who Is Different from Others

Joey, a happy, playful, 4-year-old boy diagnosed with a Pervasive Developmental Disorder (PDD), sometimes experienced difficulties in relating and communicating with peers and adults in the classroom. He enjoyed group activities, however, and often participated with Kathy's help. Joey had trouble articulating his words clearly and tended to mumble when he spoke to others in the classroom. However, he seemed to have a sense of what he wanted to say and to be quite determined to say it, and he seemed pleased with having the children respond to his expressions, as shown in the example below.

Joey now has the microphone and says something into it about how he likes to play with Power Rangers, but his words are quiet and mumbled. Kathy tells him, "I can't hear," and gets up to assist and show Joey how to hold the microphone. He repeats what he says, and Kathy, his teacher, repeats his words again for all the children.

Kathy had introduced a battery-operated toy microphone to the group for "Chat Time." She passed it around the circle so each child could have a chance to speak or sing into it, sharing something of his or her own choosing with the group. This small addition to the daily circle time not only attracted the children's interest, but it also provided amplification to those with quieter voices in the group.

Playful Community Builder with High Expectations for Collaboration: Kathy

Kathy was a fairly new teacher with 1 year of previous experience, who felt strongly about the importance of social development for the young children in her classroom. It was common practice for Kathy to join the children at the lunch table and engage them in conversation, defining this time as social in nature. Kathy asked questions and, if the children gave silly responses, she played along. She very naturally used a lot of humor to engage the children in conversation. In her interactions with the children, Kathy provided support for their ideas and initiations, even when they might be considered "inappropriate." Kathy appeared to know Joey well and to understand and anticipate those things that would make his day go more smoothly. She was often observed to interpret his words and help give meaning to his actions for the other children. Most of the time she did this through collaborating with him rather than by overtly directing his behavior, as shown in the anecdote below.

> Children are getting ready for circle time by sitting down on the chairs. Joey walks straight to a big chair, one of the classroom chairs that was somewhat larger than a typical child-sized chair. Two other children look at the big chair and walk toward it, but are one step behind Joey. Kathy notices what happens around the big chair and explains to the children "This is a special chair for Joey that will help him to be calm during our circle time. Maybe you can find another chair."

Joey had some particular rituals that he liked to honor during the classroom day. In this episode, Kathy allowed him this pleasure by ensuring that the "big chair" would be available for him. Although there were times that Joey could be misunderstood by his peers or stubborn about having his own routines despite the wishes of others, with support from his teacher he was able to fully access the classroom activities.

Joey sometimes preferred to play alone, but he had particular playmates with whom he shared reciprocal social relationships. When a child like Joey is placed in a classroom, the teacher often faces the dilemma of how to pull him into the group when he is not easily understood or sought after or doesn't initiate much. Some teachers would say, "You are reinforcing his perseveration, his ritualistic behaviors by allowing him to engage in them in the classroom." But Kathy seemed to convey the message, "I want him to be a part of the group, so I will allow him to sit on the big chair so that he will want to participate." On some level, perhaps Kathy knew that if she didn't allow Joey this special choice, she would lose him as a participant in the group. She made her decision by putting community involvement ahead of the rules or traditional assessments of appropriateness of specific behaviors. In fact, she engaged the other children in supporting Joey's use of the special chair, creating an atmosphere of collaboration rather than one of competition. Kathy demonstrated through her everyday actions in the classroom that equal is not always equitable as she negotiated how to balance meeting the needs of the group with honoring individual differences.

Kathy's Responses to Joey

Kathy approached classroom dilemmas in ways that upheld respect for children's sense of who they were and what they needed.

Individual children were not singled out as having special needs in ways that marginalized them. Kathy took a further step to create a curriculum that embraced all the learners in her classroom and brought them together in socially inclusive ways without undermining equity in experience and opportunity. However, some of the decisions Kathy made were nonconventional, such as her way of handling Joey's special chair. We see this as a meaningful choice and suggest that her ways of making these kinds of decisions in her day-to-day practice have much to teach us about creating an inclusive classroom. This story may make some teachers feel uncomfortable because they might think that it is not fair for other children when Joey always gets the special chair. They may ask, "Why wouldn't other children want to sit in that chair at circle time too?" Sometimes, notions of fairness are very rigid and concrete in early childhood classrooms, where teachers stick firmly to the rule that "everybody gets one or the same."

The following strategies could also be applied in this scenario:

Strategy 1: Other children could be invited to support Joey's use of the special chair by engaging in collaborative problem solving about other times that they could use the chair.

Strategy 2: The group could talk together about the ways that different children are most comfortable at circle time. For example, some may need to sit closer to the teacher, some prefer the rug to a chair, and some like to hold a small toy in their hand to help them listen.

This story helps us raise questions that push teachers to reflect on their own notions of fairness and to think further about the decisions they would make within a similar classroom scenario based on their goals for the children and their own points of view. Fairness is not about giving the same things to all children; rather, it is about providing equal access to opportunities that will meet the unique and diverse needs of each individual child.

FINAL WORDS: BRIDGING DEVELOPMENTAL DIFFERENCES

The children presented in our stories—Mario, Adam, and Joey—each had been identified with particular developmental delays. The nature of their delays created dilemmas for their teachers, who had to make adaptations based on the children's special needs in order to fully include them in the classroom community. The three teachers—Aurelia,

Jenny, and Kathy—were committed to making adaptations to meet the children where they were cognitively, physically, and socially. Jenny sought to provide physical assistance for Adam so that he could realize his desire to move independently, while Aurelia and Kathy tried to find ways to support social play between children with different needs and abilities. All of these teachers have developed strong interpersonal connections with their students that help them feel valued in the classroom. However, a more fundamental issue that we believe must be addressed is the need for these teachers to bridge the developmental differences between the children in their classrooms so that all of the children can experience being valuable members of the classroom community. In the process of reaching this goal, these teachers faced certain dilemmas. All of them needed to figure out how they could comfortably create this bridge for children.

We introduced three classroom components that we believe can make a difference for young children in inclusive settings and described how each component can be translated into practice to create a more meaningful inclusive experience. When discussing multiple ways to be engaged in teaching and learning (Component 1), a takeaway message from Mario's social experience is that it is not enough simply to embrace differences; teachers need to take one step further. The next step is to foster more meaningful social participation of children with special needs even when they may not be able to engage in more complex understandings. Finding the right balance in activities that are truly inclusive can be challenging. Of course it is important to give Jane the problem-solving opportunities she is ready for. But too often teachers are so focused on bringing children to the next level that they miss the opportunity to help children appreciate the value of simpler activities that they can initiate and sustain together on their own. Sometimes teachers set children up for failure by raising the stakes for activities in ways that make simpler approaches to play less valued.

In Adam's story we discussed how important it is for opportunities for interpersonal connections for all members of the community to be built into the structure of the day (Component 2). Physical environments need to be adapted not only to honor an individual child's experience but also to integrate his or her experience into the fabric of the classroom activity. At times, this adaptation may be as simple as moving an activity from one corner of the room to another. Finally, Component 3 addresses ways that the environment is designed to consider children's different ways of being and doing. In Joey's story his choice of a special chair was embraced by his teacher, without giving him or his peers the message that his behavior was perceived as atypical or strange. His feelings were validated, and he was given opportunities to connect to others. Kathy created a social bridge between Joey and other children. Kathy's choices for when and how to intervene reflected a constant consciousness about creating harmony and respect in the group. Her decisions fostered caring for others without sacrificing children's self-esteem. She made those decisions based on context rather than "rules" alone, and conveyed this deeper meaning to the children through her social connections with them.

In reality, there will be times when not all children are able to fully participate in a given task. A critical question is how teachers can help other children see that children with special needs have something valuable to offer even though their contributions may look and feel different. As discussed in the beginning of this chapter, most research on the social competencies and experiences of young children with disabilities has focused on differences in particular "normative" aspects of social interactions. Our stories seek to present a more holistic picture of social experiences in early childhood classrooms. In addition to providing alternative strategies that are aligned to each component, the following sets of questions are provided as a means to further reflect on other ways that each component can be translated into practice to create a meaningful inclusive experience.

HOW CAN YOU MAKE A DIFFERENCE? QUESTIONS FOR FURTHER REFLECTION

Mario's story

- To what extent do you believe that Aurelia is recognizing Mario as an equal contributor in the sandbox scenario? What does her response to Jane communicate about the way she values Mario's ability to engage in a meaningful interaction?
- If you were in Aurelia's shoes, how could you create an experience for Mario and Jane that would highlight Mario's interest and ability?

Adam's story

- Movement and mobility are an especially important part of daily experience for children with physical disabilities because of their physical limitations. Rather than focusing too much on how long it takes Adam to get to an activity, it is important to make movement an integrated part of his experience. Can you think of some other ways that Adam's movement can become a more integrated and valuable part of his classroom experience?

• Which of these strategies do you think would make Adam's experience more inclusive: (1) involving other children in the movement activities that he is a part of, or (2) creating an actual curriculum activity that is about moving toward something? How are these strategies different?

Joey's story

• Is there another way that Kathy could respond to Joey? What would you do differently? What are your own perspectives and feelings about allowing a child to keep his or her particular rituals, even though they may seem inappropriate at times?

• Do you think it is unfair for Joey to have the special chair all the time? In your own experiences, what notions about fairness, sharing, and cooperation do you bring to the table?

CHAPTER 3

Rethinking Social Inclusion

Classroom Components That Empower All Children

T HE PREVIOUS CHAPTER focused on teachers' challenges and opportunities as they tried to bridge developmental differences and abilities between children with special needs and their peers. The three children profiled were liked by others, including the teachers, and very rarely displayed aggressive or challenging behaviors. In this chapter we illustrate another kind of classroom quandary: how early childhood classrooms can be better equipped to respond to issues that make social inclusion more challenging. When children with developmental delays demonstrate behaviors that are socially inappropriate, different from teachers' expectations, or unacceptable to their peers, what can teachers do to make a difference? This chapter explores some possible ways to "think outside the box" that can help teachers to translate new ideas into meaningful actions that empower children with different social communication styles to become more valued members of the classroom community.

WHAT RESEARCHERS SAY ABOUT SOCIAL INCLUSION OF CHILDREN WITH CHALLENGING BEHAVIORS

Early childhood classrooms, like other communities, are social environments where different individuals with diverse personalities and a wide range of abilities come together to create a complex web of human relationships. Each classroom, in a sense, creates its own social culture within which social issues arise, such as who is included and who is excluded, who is accepted and who is rejected, and who is a powerful leader and who is a marginalized bystander. Several researchers have explored these issues within the context of children's peer relations. Traditional studies in this area focus primarily on labeling and categorizing specific characteristics of relationships. Within the social psychology tradition, researchers have focused on typologies of children's social acceptance (e.g., popular, neglected, rejected, controversial, average), various types of friendships and social relationships (e.g., acquaintance encounters, unilateral relationships, just friends, good friends, best friends), levels of social structure (e.g., social interactions, mutual friendships, peer networks, cliques), and the functions that children's friendships serve (e.g., companionship, intimacy and affection, emotional support, social comparison) (Buysse et al., 2002; Gordon, Feldman, & Chiriboga, 2005).

Children with disabilities have frequently been the subject of studies that take a more in-depth look at friendships and social rejection in peer groups. Most often, they are viewed as having limited peer-related competencies, a fact that hinders their ability to develop friendships (Guralnick, Neville, et al., 2007). For example, in a study by Lee, Yoo, and Bak (2003), peers reported that children with mild mental retardation and learning disabilities had behavioral and communication issues that interfered with building friendships. Although one study showed that children with disabilities enrolled in an integrated child care center were more likely to have at least one friend compared to their counterparts in self-contained special education classrooms (Buysse et al., 2002), Estell and colleagues (2008) suggest that inclusive environments per se (i.e., without specific social supports) may not have a beneficial effect on social acceptance even over extended periods of time.

Rejection appears to occur at a higher percentage for children with disabilities, and is a barrier for them to successful inclusion (Odom, Zercher, Marquart, et al., 2002). Children identified as socially rejected were shown to lack the skills necessary for making friends, were disruptive in class, had conflicts with peers, and tended to withdraw from social interaction or to prefer adult interaction to playing with peers. Children identified with learning disabilities also tended to have higher rates of social isolation (Wiener & Schneider, 2002), to retain fewer friendships over time, and to be more likely to have friends who also had learning disabilities, even though they were placed in inclusion settings (Estell et al., 2009). Furthermore, children's friendship preferences have been shown to vary by disability types; children with labels such as mental retardation, mental illness, and severe disabilities are rated with less approval and greater discomfort by peers (Martin, Pescosolido, & Tuch, 2000).

A few studies have taken a deeper look at children's inclusion in and exclusion from the peer culture in classrooms, delving into the issue of how power dynamics play out in early childhood classrooms.

Teachers are in a more ambiguous position as power shifts are shared and negotiated with children (Berry, 2006; Lee & Recchia, 2008). Using a theoretical framework focused on various types of community involvement—center, periphery, or margin—Berry (2006) examined power relationships in the classroom, as well as connections between classroom practice and dominant or competing traditions or discourses. Berry's study described how a child with special needs can be marginalized by typically developing peers who have stronger verbal skills that help place them in a more central role in the classroom. Although these more verbal, typically developing children sometimes include children with disabilities in activities, they can also exercise their power over others by designating particular roles in play, such that children with disabilities are left on the margins.

Below we tell the stories of children with developmental delays who demonstrate behaviors that are socially inappropriate, different from teachers' expectations, or unacceptable to their peers. Our goal is to move beyond a linear way of conceptualizing "problematic" behaviors to address the underlying issue involved in perceiving and accepting all children as integral members of an early childhood classroom community. As in the previous chapter, each component will be used as a framework to discuss social inclusion. The following components will be addressed in this chapter:

Component 4. *Children's individual differences are integrated as value-added components of the curriculum, rather than viewed as interferences or hindrances.*

In order to create early childhood classrooms that truly include and embrace all children in the community, the issues of power and inclusion in and exclusion from peer culture need to be brought to the surface. When certain children are marginalized and rejected by peers, teachers need to encourage all children to reflect upon the situation and assess it through their own eyes, rather than imposing an artificial rule, such as "we have to be nice to our friends," which may not truly reflect the children's feelings and relationships. Teachers need to feel comfortable enough to openly address exclusivity, rather than ignoring it to keep their classroom routines in place. It is all too easy to miss the opportunity to articulate how some children are being left out of the conversation. Although individual children's shortcomings may need to be acknowledged, teachers who create a socially inclusive environment for a group of diverse children need to find ways to ensure that all of the children's contributions to the classroom community are visible and respected. This may require teachers to reframe their definitions of *difference* in order to rethink the social value of children's potential contributions to the classroom community.

> Component 5. *All kinds of students are accepted and respected as important and integral members of the classroom community.*

This component addresses ways of creating an environment where all the children are included and wanted. In many schools particular children are denied enrollment in an inclusion classroom because their behaviors are not deemed socially appropriate (Gilliam & Shahar, 2006). Less emphasis is placed on the value of social inclusion when children are aggressive or display behaviors that are extremely challenging. Before agreeing with statements such as "this child does not belong" or "this child needs to be in a more restrictive environment," we want to consider multiple ways of making changes in a classroom to accommodate all of its members. Instead of setting criteria for who "fits in" the inclusion classroom, we want to think creatively about ways to make the classroom environment a better fit for all the children, including those who didn't seem to fit within the previously set criteria. Each child's motivation, social skills, interests, and levels of social engagement need to be honored and supported.

> Component 6. *Support is provided for young children with a wide array of skills, abilities, strengths, and needs, to help them reach their full potential.*

It is very easy for teachers to pay attention to those children who are verbally expressive and place themselves into the foreground. Teachers' attention is also monopolized by those who are disruptive and present challenging behaviors. As a result, children who are shy and on the periphery can fall under the radar, and their value to the group is not always recognized. When thinking about providing supports to children, it is important for teachers to remember those who are quiet and seem less able to anchor themselves to peers. For these children, developing strong relationships with teachers may need to take precedence, as the teacher–child connection can serve as their passageway into becoming a part of the group (Howes & Hamilton, 1992; Recchia & Dvorakova, 2012).

IRA'S STORY:
DEALING WITH A CHILD WHO IS
MARGINALIZED IN THE CLASSROOM

This story highlights Component 4: *Children's individual differences are integrated as value-added components of the curriculum rather than viewed as interferences or hindrances.* Rejection by peers in classroom settings is a barrier to successful inclusion for preschool children with disabilities. Children who are socially rejected sometimes engage in substantially less positive interaction or substantially more negative interaction with peers than other children (Odom, Zercher, Marquart, et al., 2002). These children may lack the skills necessary for making friends. This story is about Ira, who was often rejected by popular children in the classroom and raises the issue of exclusion from the peer culture in inclusion classrooms.

An Integrated Preschool Classroom

Ira was a 4-year-old boy attending the preschool classroom of a university-affiliated child care center in New York City (see Table 1.1 for background information). The center provided a primarily child-centered, play-based curriculum. The classroom served a mixed-age group of 3- to 5-year-old children and followed an emergent curriculum philosophy. There were approximately 14 children, 2 head teachers, and several assistant teachers in the classroom. The children's day included a long period of free play when they could engage with any of the materials in the classroom that they chose. Many of the children enjoyed varieties of fantasy play during this time. Because of the range of ages and skills, most activities took on a flexible nature, allowing children to engage in different ways and at levels that were appropriate to their needs, interests, and abilities.

The classroom children demonstrated a wide range of competencies. However, three of these children, Calvin, Louis, and Jackie, stood out as "leaders" in the group because of their strong personalities and powerful presence (Lee & Recchia, 2008). Throughout the year, the teachers had been struggling with issues of social justice in the classroom, which often arose in the context of the powerful roles that these young leaders held among their peers. Calvin and Louis could be very exclusive in their play, and Jackie had so much to say that she often left little room for others to share their ideas.

A Preschooler with Special Needs Under the Shadow of Dominant, Typically Developing Peers

Ira was one of the few children with special needs in this integrated preschool classroom. He had mild developmental delays (without a specific diagnosis). When Ira first arrived in the classroom, his parents made no mention of his developmental delays nor shared any concerns they had regarding his development. But as he spent more time in this classroom, his teachers began to notice his delays. After consultation with his parents, Ira was eventually referred for an evaluation which resulted in his receiving special education services through a Special Education Itinerant Teacher (SEIT). During the evaluation process, the teachers were informed that Ira had had a mild stroke shortly after birth. Ira was able to participate in all the classroom activities, but careful observation of his behavior showed his developmental delays in cognitive processing and pragmatic use of language.

Ira was socially aware and showed a preference for other boys. He tended to play with younger children and needed the teacher's assistance when involved in complex play with peers his own age. He liked to listen to storybooks and engage in simple, repetitive activities. He tended to move from one activity to another without further developing a complex play scenario. Although Ira was recognized by his peers, he was not fully integrated into the social environment of this classroom. He was often ignored by the other children in the classroom, and his voice was frequently left unheard. Ira showed a special interest in Calvin, a dynamic, outgoing, and charismatic classroom leader whose creative sense of humor was quite attractive to other children. However, Calvin did not reciprocate Ira's initiations, as shown in the following anecdote:

> While playing with LEGOs at the table, Calvin and Ira say repeatedly to each other, "No." Calvin turns around and voices his discontentment. He walks up to the teacher and tells on Ira, whom he says is not sharing. The teacher says, "Ira, you can share the LEGOs." Ira says, "It's for everybody." Then Calvin says, "He thinks I'm not everybody!" Calvin is still not happy. He gets up and moves closer to his friend, away from Ira.

Teacher Support for Children's Classroom Leadership: Beverly and Reah

The two teachers in this classroom, Beverly and Reah, had several years of previous experience with this age group. They described themselves as teachers who were "pretty fair," "funny," and "willing to respond to children's individual needs." They wanted to work on building an early childhood classroom community with an emphasis on social and emotional development. Even when the teachers were able to envision ways to facilitate an ideal social environment where all children, including those from diverse backgrounds and with a wide range of abilities, can have equal social opportunities and share power, the everyday challenges they faced with the real children in their classrooms made it difficult at times to bring their visions to life. For example, teachers may inadvertently empower some children while disenfranchising others in the ways that they encourage or discourage particular classroom behaviors. Consider the following instance:

> "Calvin, Calvin, Calvin," Ira calls. "I'm talking to you, Calvin!" Calvin does not respond to Ira. Instead, Calvin reaches over and takes a Spider-Man cup from Harry, who quickly turns to look at him.
>
> Calvin smiles and puts it back. Harry smiles.
>
> "Calvin, Calvin." Ira looks directly at Calvin, waving a large plastic bottle of orange juice in front of him while calling his name. Calvin does not look up.
>
> Calvin leans toward Harry, who is sitting on his right, and says something.
>
> Harry smiles as Calvin speaks.
>
> Ira calls out again, "Calvin! Talk to me!"
>
> Calvin replies quietly without looking up, "No."
>
> Ira asks Calvin, "Do you use the bathroom?"
>
> "Stop it!" Calvin replies. "I don't want to talk to you."
>
> "Calvin, Calvin," Ira calls again, waving his juice.
>
> Beverly intercedes. "Calvin is not being such a good friend to you right now. Show someone else who's interested," she tells Ira.
>
> "Calvin," he continues.
>
> "OK. OK," Calvin says, looking up. "I'm not talking to you."

As shown in the anecdote above, Calvin often excluded Ira from his play. He openly ignored Ira's attempt to initiate play with him, while he showed a friendly response to Harry, one of his special friends. When Calvin expressed his like/dislike toward peers such as Ira through his powerful communication, it was quite obvious who was in and out of his inner circle. We noticed how the teacher inadvertently put the responsibility on Ira to solve his social problems. The teacher asked him to find someone who could be nice to him. This approach makes Ira responsible to find a nicer friend, while Calvin, who excluded Ira from play, is free of responsibility.

The Interaction Between Ira and Calvin at the Lunch Table

In the scenario described above, because of the special friendships that Calvin had with a few of the other classroom boys, the issue of exclusion/inclusion often became more obvious when they excluded particular children such as Ira from their play. At the lunch table, the teacher allowed Calvin to choose to ignore Ira by redirecting Ira rather than requiring Calvin to respond to him. The teacher did not openly address the way that Calvin was excluding Ira. In situations like this, a better alternative may be to acknowledge children's shortcomings and try to respect their contribution to the classroom community. Instead of asking children to be polite or look for another nice friend, teachers need to encourage children to reflect upon the given situation and assess it through their own eyes. It is important for the teachers to feel comfortable with openly addressing exclusivity, instead of primarily focusing on keeping the routine flowing. It is too easy to ignore the opportunity to articulate how some children can be marginalized. When teachers see children from a deficit-oriented perspective, they may not realize the ways that their views can impact the messages they give to other children in the classroom. As powerful classroom role models, teachers can set the tone in their classrooms for how children will be valued by others through implementing strategies like these:

Strategy 1: More explicit instructions or proactive strategies can be taught to Ira so that he can approach Calvin in a more socially appropriate way. This type of strategy would demonstrate the teacher's support of Ira and help him to have a more effective voice in the classroom.

Strategy 2: The teacher could sit down with Calvin and discuss how he could respond to Ira without being mean or exclusive toward him. This would encourage Calvin to take responsibility for his actions and to gain more insight into the impact of his behavior on others.

Strategy 3: Some special activities could be created that would bring the boys together through a shared experience. For example, maybe Calvin and Ira could be asked to work as a team to accomplish a classroom task to which Ira could make a significant contribution. In some ways, these children need to be given unique opportunities that separate them from the group because it is unlikely that Calvin would be naturally motivated to play with Ira if there are other competing options. This might require some scaffolding on the teachers' part in order to create an opportunity for Calvin to see Ira in a different light.

This story tells us how the power dynamics in the classroom can have a meaningful impact on social relationships and ways of building an inclusive social community. Early childhood teachers often ignore the idea of power dynamics, missing opportunities to raise critical questions about teachers' and children's behaviors. In order to create early childhood classroom communities that truly embrace diversity and empower all children to find their voices, teachers need to make a conscious effort to bring issues of power in from the shadows by articulating them with and for young children. One of the teachers' crucial roles is to reflect upon when and how to support children to be empowered.

CODY'S STORY:
RESPONDING TO AN AGGRESSIVE CHILD

This story highlights Component 5: *All kinds of students are accepted and respected as important and integral members of the classroom community.* Children who are aggressive and/or violent present particular challenges to creating inclusive classroom communities. Their behaviors can shift the focus from supporting social inclusion to maintaining safety. Cody's story raises questions regarding whether there are limits to who gets to be included, particularly when a child's behavior can be potentially harmful to others. Some people may say, "This child doesn't belong in an inclusion classroom. It is not fair to the other kids." When thinking about children who display challenging behaviors, we attempt to move beyond simply focusing on behavior management strategies to finding ways to reframe perspectives on how aggressive children can be included with others in the classroom.

An Integrated Early Childhood Education Classroom: Inclusion Within a Specialized Setting

Cody's classroom was an integrated preschool room for children between 3 and 5 years old, housed within a special education center that provided a full continuum of services, including several self-contained preschool classrooms. There were 9 children enrolled in the class, 5 of whom were receiving special education services and 4 who were not. The group was originally envisioned as an alternative setting to the more traditional self-contained classrooms at the site, and the children selected for this classroom had well-developed language and play skills.

Camille worked with two assistants in the classroom, and frequently a speech or occupational therapist also participated in classroom activities. The curriculum was primarily play-based, and included time for free play each day. In addition, there was a circle time where children engaged in a series of songs and activities on a regular basis and a time each day to play on the rooftop playground. Camille also introduced many creative group activities for the children to participate in, such as making lemonade from fresh lemons and designing their own graduation hats. Most often Camille was a very calm and centered presence in the classroom, and it seemed that the children had come to depend on her for help in maintaining classroom equilibrium. Camille was exceptionally good at explaining things to the children and preparing them for what would happen next.

Many of the children were able to anticipate classroom routines and engage in daily activities easily. However, there was a small group of children in this classroom, including Cody, who could quickly push each others' buttons, setting off a negative chain of behavior that could make the classroom atmosphere emotionally charged in ways that were very challenging for the teachers to manage.

A Social, Energetic Preschooler with Intense Emotional Responses

Cody, a bright, physically active, and socially aware 3½-year-old boy, exuded energy in a way that made it hard to keep his hands to himself. He enjoyed participating with the group in social activities, but at times it seemed that his enthusiasm could become overwhelming to both himself and others. Consider the following anecdote:

Michael is at the front, then Cody. Cody hits at Michael's head slightly. Sandy (assistant teacher) says, "Cody, you can put your hands on the chair instead of on his head." Cody complies. He participates, smiling and singing along with the "Wheels on the Bus" song. He uses appropriate gestures and motions. When his teacher, Camille, rewinds the tape and it makes a loud, funny sound, the children giggle, including Cody. He is ready for the next action. Donny gets up, and Cody pushes him, saying, "Sit down!" Donny does. Camille says, "Cody, you can tell him without touching him." Cody says, "I'm not Cody, I'm the bus driver." Then the music plays again and they all return to having fun together.

Cody was highly sensitive to the other children's behavior and often placed himself in the role of "policing" his friends. Sometimes his eagerness to enforce the rules or his version of social order resulted in his becoming overly aggressive toward his peers.

Although Cody could demonstrate lots of positive engagement in classroom activities on some days, there were other days when he arrived at school in a bad mood. On these days, it was hard for Camille to help him engage in classroom activities.

Cody was leaning against the bookrack in the children's circle area still wearing his backpack and baseball cap, refusing to take them off. It is apparent that Camille has been trying to coax Cody out of his "blue funk." "In one minute I will help you get ready," she says. Cody answers with a long, wailing "Noooo." Camille says, "One minute," and leaves the room.

When responding to Cody's challenging behaviors, Camille seemed especially tuned in to Cody, and it was clear that he was able to rely on her for help quite often when things started to become out of control.

The children are playing musical chairs. Cody crawls around with the others, smiling and squealing. They are pretending to be different animals as they find their chairs. Now they are jumping like frogs. Camille models how they can say, "Don't scream, it hurts my ears." When Cody goes to his chair, Camille says, "Good not screaming, Cody!"

A few of the other children in the group also struggled with emotion regulation issues and could easily get caught up with Cody in an escalating negative behavioral spiral. Although he had particular playmates within the classroom and the capacity to interact with his friends in very socially appropriate ways, sometimes Cody seemed physically and emotionally unable to stay calm enough to benefit from being included in the group. Cody's strong and overriding interest in being a member of the group was highly motivating for him. However, within the group context it was exceptionally difficult for him to regain his calm once he was riled up.

Teacher Support for Children's Social and Coping Skills: Camille

Stating her most effective teaching strategy to be modeling appropriate behaviors and using everyday opportunities in order to "show children how to say, do, and act appropriately," Camille worked hard to enact her beliefs in her classroom practice. She was highly attentive to the children's behavior and tried to be consistent and supportive in her responses to them.

Camille believed that her least effective strategy was "reacting too quickly to certain situations." Given the ways that some of the children's emotions could quickly cycle out of control in her classroom, she had many opportunities to practice not doing this. However, sometimes when Cody's negative behavior escalated very quickly in ways that could be threatening to the other children, Camille was quick to separate him from the others until he was able to become calm again, as in the following anecdote.

> The group has begun singing the "Hello" song, but there are many interruptions. It is hard for several of the children to stay focused. When Cody asks to participate in a particular way, Camille tells him calmly that this is not a choice this morning. Cody immediately picks up his chair and throws it across the room. At this point, Camille moves the circle out of the classroom into the hallway, leaves her assistant in charge of the group, and returns to help Cody calm down until he is ready to rejoin the group.

Camille and her assistant, Sandy, had been exploring ways to help Cody regain his equilibrium when he fell apart in the group. On this day they were trying out a new strategy. Rather than having Cody leave the group, they found that having the group exit to the hallway, leaving him in the classroom alone, seemed to be a more effective way to give him the message that he could not participate in the fun things with others unless he could control his behavior. When he acted out in inappropriate ways, he would literally be left behind.

With Camille's help, and in a calm and quiet atmosphere, Cody could usually regain his equilibrium and resume group participation within a relatively short time.

Camille's Responses to Cody's Meltdown

In many early childhood classrooms, when there are disruptive behaviors, teachers take a child out of the group, using a time-out. But in this case, Camille took the group away from the child. Too often, children like Cody are not welcomed into or are referred out of a setting. It is hard for children who are aggressive and/or violent to be integral members of the community, and sometimes these children are perceived as a threat to the safety of the classroom. In Cody's case, we believe that the inclusive classroom was a potentially effective environment for him since he was so motivated to be with his peers. The particular strategy of leaving Cody behind may seem to go against traditional early childhood philosophy. It must have been scary for Cody to be the only one in the room when he was usually there with the whole group. When this strategy was used, Cody was all alone, and everyone else had gone off to do some fun things from which he was excluded. He couldn't necessarily predict what was going on because it was a break from the daily routine. Instead of just focusing on addressing Cody's aggressive behaviors, different strategies could be used to create more opportunities for his inclusive experience.

> *Strategy 1:* Cody's motivation to be part of the group must be thought about carefully when planning strategies for him. His aggression may be a way of communicating and trying to relate to or get attention from the group. Instead of just reacting to control his behaviors, his teachers need to weigh the positives and negatives of particular intervention strategies from this perspective. For example, finding appropriate ways to involve Cody as a group leader, before aggression appears, might allow him to channel his energy in a more positive way.
>
> *Strategy 2:* Teachers need to assess Cody's strengths and weaknesses. Because he is so physically active, his teachers may need to allocate more time within the day when the children can be engaged in physical activity as an integral part of the curriculum. Changes need to be made in the classroom to better accommodate Cody, so that he can use his strengths to more consistently be a part of the group's social experiences.

In this story, Camille supported Cody's appropriate participation in the group whenever possible because she was aware of Cody's strong social interest in playing with the other children and being a part of the classroom activities. She fostered his ability to self-regulate so that he could be included, but at times this could only be accomplished by excluding Cody from the group. Rather than allow Cody to disrupt other children's involvement in playful learning activities, Camille and her assistants would leave him behind as the others moved to another space to continue with their fun. This plan seemed to help articulate for Cody and for all the children that behavior that was threatening to others was not acceptable and could not be tolerated. This strategy had a long-term impact that helped Cody change his behavior in a more meaningful way.

ABIGAIL'S STORY: ATTENDING TO A QUIET CHILD WHO DOES NOT DEMAND THE TEACHERS' ATTENTION

Children who feel shy or tend to stay on the periphery often seem to be floating on the outskirts of social activity, watching the group without raising their voices. It is important to provide opportunities for these children to interact in small groups with supportive peers in order to bolster their confidence and comfort level (Kemple, 2004). This story addresses how children at the margin need to be supported so that they don't fall through the cracks. This story illustrates Component 6: *Support is provided for young children with a wide array of skills, abilities, strengths, and needs, to help them reach their full potential.*

An Integrated Prekindergarten Classroom Within a Specialized Setting

Abigail's classroom was an integrated prekindergarten room for children between 3½ and 5 years old, located in a special education program that provided a full continuum of services, including several self-contained preschool classrooms. There were 16 children enrolled in the class, half of whom were receiving special education services. The curriculum for this classroom was designed to prepare the children for kindergarten and to enhance the readiness skills of those with special needs to help them to be more eligible for a placement in an inclusive kindergarten setting.

Mary, whose background was in special education, and Lorna, whose background was in general education, worked as co-head teachers, running the classroom with the help of Omar, their assistant teacher. Several of the children in the classroom were emergent bilinguals, with Spanish as their home language, and Omar's bilingual skills were often put to good use.

The daily activities followed a schedule that included time for large- and small-group work. The children engaged in many hands-on activities, for which the adults provided scaffolding. Each day included literacy activities such as story time, and the children were often invited to be participants in "teaching" the group. The teachers often brought materials into the classroom to create hands-on learning opportunities for the children, such as making mud with soil and water, and exploring the taste, smell, and texture of mangos. The children also made use on a daily basis of the large, on-site gymnasium, which was well equipped with riding toys, large and small balls, and other equipment that supported gross-motor activity.

The majority of children in this classroom were able to readily engage with the classroom activities although they demonstrated diverse skill levels. There were clear expectations in place for appropriate behavior, and behavior was monitored each day with the use of a chart marking "good behavior stamps" for each of five activity periods throughout the day. Children, particularly those who were out of line, were reminded about their behavior on a regular basis. Teachers clearly articulated that behavioral compliance was valued in the classroom.

A Quiet, Enthusiastic, Observant Preschooler Who Speaks Louder with Her Body Than with Her Voice

Abigail, a physically active but verbally quiet 3½-year-old girl, was often an onlooker in her classroom. Throughout our observations, we saw Abigail attending to many activities, watching as others shared their ideas, and occasionally engaging in very brief verbal exchanges with adults and peers. However, during typical large-group activities, it was much more common for Abigail to say nothing at all than to even utter a few participatory words. Although she did attend to the classroom activities with some interest, there were times when it seemed very apparent that it was hard for her to do so without fidgeting. She had a tendency to play with her mouth, cheeks, and face as she participated in large-group sessions. Sometimes she squirmed and wiggled into new positions as she tried to sit through circle time in the classroom. The following two anecdotes show Abigail's typical ways of engaging in classroom activities.

Abigail looks toward Nora (speech therapist), watching attentively as she reads to the group. Nora has a book about a dinosaur. Abigail sits looking at the book. As Nora reads the back of the book to give the children a hint about the story, many of the children ask questions, but Abigail is quiet. She holds her face in her hands, watches, and listens to others. After a few minutes she puts her head down, kind of rocks her body a little, a little antsy, but keeps to herself and quiet.

Abigail runs her hand back and forth along the floor. She still looks toward the book and Nora though . . . she changes position, imitating Liana, who is moving onto her knees. Abigail doesn't really go into any one position; she just kind of rocks on her knees for a few minutes, then sits again.

Given a specific responsibility with an established protocol, however, Abigail seemed able to take on her role and interact with her peers more fluently. When it was her turn to be line leader, for example, she took up the task with enthusiasm.

Abigail is the line leader. Omar (assistant teacher) announces this and she goes right to the line. She encounters another child and says, "I'm line leader," reaching out to move past him and secure her position at the front of the line. She stands at the front of the line with Omar, her finger in her mouth. . . . While line leader, Abigail does her job. At one point they must stop before heading down a staircase, to wait for the others to catch up. Abigail tells the child behind her to wait. He says, "No," but she says, "Yes," several times, using a nice loud voice.

Once in the gym, Abigail showed another side of her personality. Given the freedom to move in this large open space, Abigail's spirit came to life. Her well-developed motor skills allowed her to engage in movement activities with a high level of competence, and her enthusiasm for physical activity was easily apparent. In the gym she could initiate social connections with other children, using her body as her primary means of communicating.

As soon as Abigail is told she can go play, she runs to a bike, mounts it easily, and starts to ride around the room. She goes fast, watching others. . . . She approaches Mark, and asks him to ride with her on his scooter. "Come on, let's go," she says. At first he says something like "I'm coming," but he sees a hula hoop and is distracted by it. He doesn't really ride with her. She calls out as she rides, something about a monster. Mark is running all around with the hula hoop, and he doesn't really pay attention to her. She seems happy to continue riding fast, with or without him. . . . Abigail pretends to beep her horn, then tries to engage Mark again. He ignores her, busy with his hoop. He then mounts a bike too, with his hula hoop. She comes around the bend, talking into her hand, almost as if it is a walkie-talkie. At one point she says, "Mark, come in!" Omar calls; she looks, smiles, still riding fast. She is very positive throughout this activity—she really seems to enjoy this. She continues to yell out something as she's riding fast. . . . Abigail bumps into Liana, who gets off her bike and runs, smiling playfully. This seems to be part of the game. Abigail rides on, Liana is on another bike, and they ride in a circle.

Abigail's physical competence far outweighed her verbal skills, making it hard for her to find her place in a classroom of highly verbal children. She was challenged by the verbal nature of many of the classroom activities and seemed reluctant to participate at times, even with adult scaffolding. Viewing her in other contexts, we saw that she was very capable of engaging in a wide range of playful interactions with peers, but she did this best in a setting where she had the freedom to move and explore on her own terms.

Teachers' Efforts to Prepare All Children for Kindergarten: Lorna and Mary

Lorna and Mary worked as a team to address the needs of a diverse group of children with a focus on preparing them for success in kindergarten. Although their curriculum included many preacademic skills, both teachers ranked language and social development at the top of their lists of importance. For Mary, a primary goal for the children was "to build self-esteem, independence, as well as cooperative peer and adult interactions." Lorna echoed this sentiment in her stated goal: "To begin actively engaging in the learning process in ways that promote communication, observation, and risk taking."

Although both teachers shared some common goals, each brought her own style to her interactions with the children. As the special education teacher, Mary tended to look more closely at individual differences in the children, stating her most effective teaching strategy as "giving children choices within a structured, developmentally appropriate setting (child-directed curriculum)." Lorna focused more on socially appropriate behaviors for the whole group, choosing as a least effective strategy "transitions in which children spend time waiting for just a few children."

In our observations of the teachers' interactions with Abigail, it was clear that she was given many opportunities to engage with the classroom curriculum in appropriate ways. The teachers seemed very aware of her need for support in connecting with peers and often made suggestions that pushed her toward more inclusive experiences, such as in the following example:

> Abigail sits alone while all of the other children are in groups—the girls looking together at a book and the boys at a toy. Lorna says, "Conrad, move over to where Abigail is." He does, but no interaction takes place.

However, it was often the case that these suggestions stopped short of becoming actualized appropriate peer experiences for Abigail as she was not able to follow through with the next steps without additional support. Too often in the busy classroom, another need arose, distracting the adults from Abigail's dilemma. With her silence and easy, compliant nature, Abigail did not seem to demand their attention in the ways that some other children did, and she could easily be lost on the periphery when things got hectic.

> Mary gets up to do the behavior stamps, and the children in circle start to lose attention. Abigail is popping air from one of her cheeks to the other, poking her cheeks with her fingers. She looks at her fingers before she pokes. Mary says, "Abigail, good job this morning," giving her a stamp. Abigail looks toward Mary, but her facial affect remains dull. A group of boys gathers in the center of the circle, talking about colors. Abigail stays in place, leaning back against the shelf, quiet. She yawns.

The Interactions Between Mary and Abigail

In this case, the dilemma is: What can teachers do to help Abigail take the next step in engaging with peers or in large-group activities? How is Abigail given space, support, and tools to reach her full potential? Because she is so quiet, she needs help from her teachers to create more opportunities for social engagement with other children before the classroom gets too hectic. Before teachers become fully engaged in an activity, they could take time to pay attention to Abigail's voice.

Sometimes the issue is not only about children taking more initiative, but about teachers paying closer attention to children on the margins. Teachers have to make a connection and stay with the child through full engagement to keep from losing her on the periphery. It was unlikely that Abigail would ask for the teachers' attention, so the teachers have to make special efforts to engage her as the activities begin, before other children compete with her for their attention. When teachers don't make special efforts, a child like Abigail may eventually get the message that nobody really cares what she has to say. If she realizes nobody is paying attention to her, she is less likely to be motivated to participate. She is fine doing her own thing. But if she knows that the teacher is focusing on her and has an expectation, she may be more motivated to engage. Different strategies can be used to highlight her presence in the classroom.

> *Strategy 1:* Teachers need to get to know Abigail on a more personal level, put extra effort in to figure out her agenda, and create a hook for her to be connected (e.g., more opportunities for small groups). Abigail clearly loves movement activities, for example, which could be used as a basis for her engagement in the classroom, not just in the gym.
>
> *Strategy 2:* Abigail's voice needs to be brought into the group for her peers to notice her as valuable. When setting the agenda for the group, the teachers could be more intentional about giving Abigail an opportunity to voice her opinions, instead of just listening to children who are loud and more eager to initiate in expressing their ideas.
>
> *Strategy 3:* In addition to the traditional kinds of oral discussion that take place in most early childhood classrooms, other forums could be made available through which children can convey their knowledge and interests. Privileging nonverbal modes of sharing during some group meetings or at other times of the day can create new opportunities for expression for less verbal children.

In this story we address different ways of bringing the voices of quiet children like Abigail into the group and teaching peers about their value. Small changes in teachers' behaviors can change the group dynamic and peers' awareness of group membership. Sometimes it is not enough for teachers to ask questions during circle time; they need to make it a point to call upon children who don't talk a lot, as well as invite alternative forms of expression. Also, when quiet children develop a relationship and feel safe with the teachers, they are more likely to feel comfortable enough to respond within the group with the teachers' support. Consequently, other children will be more able to see what quiet children can bring to the group. By taking small steps in changing their behaviors and intentionality, teachers can find the starting point for building an inclusive community.

FINAL WORDS: DEVELOPING NEW MIND-SETS TO PROMOTE INCLUSIVE CLASSROOMS THAT VALUE EVERYONE

For Ira, Cody, and Abigail, despite their interest in the group and their ability to engage in classroom activities, there were times when they were not naturally or peacefully included in the group, or when their behavior did not meet with their teachers' expectations. Ira's play agenda was not often welcomed by peers, especially the leaders in the classroom who clearly expressed their wish to exclude him from their inner circle. Although he often tried to gain access by saying something silly or repeating the rules, in the face of rejection he was often left powerless. Cody could easily become emotionally unstable and sometimes volatile in the classroom. When this happened, his presence could impose a risk to the other children's safety. Cody had a hard time keeping his hands to himself when he was excitedly playing with others, and what started out as a tap or a poke could soon become a more severe hit, kick, or scratch. What began as enthusiastic laughter could quickly erupt into yelling and screaming at a level that could be frightening, especially to the younger children in the group. Abigail did not take an active role in participating in the community in a way that teachers were reinforcing. When teachers were conducting the large-group activities, Abigail didn't seem to pay any attention or show interest in the teachers' agenda. She just faded into the background and didn't get noticed.

These three stories articulate how difficult it is to establish an inclusive classroom where all kinds of children are accepted and respected as important members of the classroom community. Cody's teacher Camille tried hard to create a social space for the children in her classroom that felt safe and respectful. With a strong goal of fostering inclusion, Camille tried to model for the children effective ways of communicating with each other and negotiating to solve problems. She did an excellent job of scaffolding for the children to help them anticipate what would happen and thus prepare for it. However, she could not always anticipate when Cody might act out in unsafe ways. In Ira's case, the teachers were often observed to be responding differently to children with powerful voices compared to children who were more marginalized in the group, especially children with special needs such as Ira. Abigail's teachers provided several opportunities for her to engage with peers in appropriate ways. However, their typical strategies did not seem to match Abigail's unique ways of relating to peers. In the midst of the busy classroom, Abigail's silent presence was not easily included in the community.

Including children like Ira, Cody, and Abigail requires that teachers be able to be extra sensitive to the quiet voice on the periphery, to tolerate some unexpected disruptions to their daily routines, and to find a way to be comfortable with the discomfort brought about when social relationships become challenging in their classrooms. In order to truly create opportunities for these children to be a part of the group, teachers may have to step outside of accepted models of classroom practice and even reconsider their own beliefs about what is socially appropriate. They must consider to what extent they can allow children not to follow their typical expectations and the usual protocol.

We introduced three classroom components that we believe can make a difference for children who may not be considered appropriate candidates to be placed in inclusion classrooms. Cody's story in particular raises a question about the limits of inclusion, and challenges us to think deeply about the realities of including children whose behaviors can pose a threat to others. That Camille was committed to keep trying new strategies with Cody until she found one that seemed to be effective was a testament to her strong belief in his capacity to be a fully included member of the group. Despite his challenging behaviors, she was able to stay focused on his strengths, to think creatively about ways to keep him actively interested in being a group participant, and to include him whenever possible. At the same time, she was also able to instill a sense of safety in the classroom that allowed the other children to more easily accept Cody as a classmate. In these ways, Camille provided support for increasing Cody's emotion regulation skills while also giving him a sense of belonging as a significant member of the group. This story addresses how important it is to accept and respect all kinds of children, even those with challenging behaviors, as important and integral members of the classroom community (Component 5).

Highlighting the other end of spectrum, Abigail's story brought attention to the issue of children who are excluded on the margin because they are so quiet that they don't get noticed by peers. In order to bring these children into the group, they first need to make a connection to the teachers, and their relationships with the teachers can be a bridge that connects them to peers. Support is provided for young children with a wide array of skills, abilities, strengths, and needs, to help them reach their full potential (Component 6). Although a child who does not demand teachers' attention in the ways that others do may not be seen as a "problem," she may also not be fully included in the community. Children on the periphery can create a sense of discomfort in teachers, as they are not actively engaging in what the teacher offers them in the classroom.

Ira's story raises a very critical question: When children who take on powerful leadership roles in the classroom use their status to marginalize their peers with special needs, what are the implications for building an inclusive community? As shown in the example presented above, it creates feelings of discomfort when children make choices that exclude a certain group of children, especially those with special needs. To some extent, this type of behavior can and does happen in any group setting. It is so common that it becomes easy to overlook it in a busy classroom environment and to see the child who is being ignored or left out as the problem. But each time a teacher inadvertently allows a Calvin to treat an Ira badly, she misses an opportunity to model something different for the whole group and to make a particular difference in both these children's lives. The lesson from the story is how children's individual differences are integrated as value-added components of the curriculum rather than viewed as interferences or hindrances (Component 4). Like the previous chapter, this chapter ends with three sets of questions for further reflection on other ways that each component can be translated into practice.

HOW CAN YOU MAKE A DIFFERENCE? QUESTIONS FOR FURTHER REFLECTION

Ira's story

- What can teachers say to Calvin to encourage changes in his thinking and help him take responsibility for his actions?
- Is creating opportunities/manipulating the social situation for Ira too much intervention? How comfortable would you be as the teacher in stepping in to facilitate these opportunities? Would it be better for Ira to have to figure things out on his own?

Cody's story

- What is the difference between removing the child from the group to a typical time-out and leaving the child behind? Why may this strategy be more effective for Cody? How comfortable would you be leaving a child behind in this way as the group goes on to engage in activities without him?
- Are there limits to who should be accepted into a preschool classroom? What are your feelings about school expulsion for children whose behaviors are challenging? What are your criteria for who should be accepted into an integrated preschool classroom?

Abigail's story

- What message do we give Abigail when we don't expect or ask for her participation? How can the teacher make it clear to her that she has something valuable to offer the group?
- How can the daily classroom schedule be changed so that children like Abigail who are quiet can express their thoughts outside of a typical platform such as a circle time?

CHAPTER 4

Becoming a Teacher Who Makes a Difference

Examining Values, Reconsidering Expectations, and Developing Competencies to Transform Classroom Practice

E ARLY CHILDHOOD TEACHERS who view diversity as the norm and classroom communities as inclusive (Danforth, 2006; Valle & Connor, 2011) must work with intentionality to proactively advocate for and enact inclusive practices (Hehir, 2005). This process begins with teachers' ability to see all children as active learners who have something to contribute to the group; it requires that teachers adjust their thinking to accommodate a variety of different learning styles among the children in their classrooms and to capitalize on these differences in building a classroom community; and it necessitates a change in teachers' actions to translate these new ways of thinking into everyday practice. A popular quote attributed to Mohandas Gandhi suggests that we must "be the change we wish to see in the world"; likewise, through the process of enacting inclusive practice, individual teachers can collectively transform classroom cultures.

Inclusion is conceptualized not as a place or a set of strategies, but as a state of mind translated into action. Choices made in the small moments of everyday practice anchored in deeper understandings of inclusion can have a big impact on children's experiences in the classroom. In this chapter, we discuss the challenges of inclusion and the important role of reflective thinking as a first step toward changing practice. We also present six teacher competencies that can make a difference in building an inclusive classroom community. As we describe them, we return to classroom examples presented in Chapters 2 and

3, rethinking possible teacher actions to illuminate new possibilities for inclusive practice.

CHALLENGES OF INCLUSION

In their recently published joint position statement on inclusion, the Division for Early Childhood (DEC) of the Council for Exceptional Children and the National Association for the Education of Young Children (NAEYC) (DEC/NAEYC, 2009) came together to establish a clear statement on the meaning and practice of early childhood inclusion. They articulated three primary areas that are essential components of inclusion: access, participation, and support. Although the proliferation of both scholarly and popular literature addressing issues of inclusion might lead us to believe that access to inclusive programs has dramatically increased in recent years, in their recent analysis of inclusive practice in early childhood, Odom, Buysse, and Soukakou (2011) found that there has been much less progress than expected in the past decade in placing young children with disabilities in inclusive classrooms. Successful inclusion, according to these authors, has much more to do with collaboration among adults than with addressing particular disabilities in children. They suggest that the most promising strategies for change will come about through "innovations that fundamentally change current structures and ways of thinking about program quality to ensure that each and every child succeeds" (p. 351).

According to Odom et al. (2011), high-quality inclusion is about belonging and membership, positive social relationships and friendships, and development and learning, rather than a type of placement; and, most importantly, it must be conceptualized for all children, not just those with disabilities. Inclusive communities are best established and sustained when key stakeholders, including parents, teachers, administrators, and policy makers, have a shared vision that is supported by state and national policies, professional preparation programs, and organizational structures. Kemple (2004) also describes the need to consider multiple factors in creating and sustaining effective inclusive programs. These factors include overall program quality, knowledge and skills of teachers, and the degree to which the curriculum is innovative and responsive. Although we have been talking in the field about inclusive practice for quite some time, there is still much work to be done to address the establishment of inclusive opportunities for young children with special needs.

Barriers to inclusion continue to persist, in part due to what Strain, Schwartz, and Barton (2011) refer to as "inclusion myths." These include the "readiness myth," which assumes that children can only be in inclusive classrooms after they have mastered particular milestones; the "tutorial instruction myth," which assumes that children with particular disabilities such as autism can only learn through one-on-one direct instruction; the "overstimulation myth," which assumes that the inclusive classroom is overstimulating in ways that bring on children's problem behaviors; and the "behavioral control limitation myth," which assumes that severe behavior problems can only be treated in restrictive settings. These authors encourage teachers, administrators, and policy makers to consider "quality of life" issues for young children and their families by creating inclusive programs that help children develop the skills they need to become higher functioning members of their families and communities.

The promise of inclusion rests largely on the shoulders of those who are positioned to effect changes in the current system. Early childhood teachers hold powerful positions in young children's lives, serving as both their role models and their advocates. Because they are working with children who are still developing their sense of themselves as social beings, early childhood teachers are poised to have a lasting impact on young children's long-term development of interpersonal competencies with peers. These emergent competencies, such as peer group entry, conflict resolution, and maintaining play, have been "directly associated with later quality of life issues involving independence, self-determination, and inclusion" (Guralnick, 2010, p. 81).

WHAT RESEARCHERS SAY ABOUT THE ROLE OF TEACHERS IN FACILITATING SOCIAL INTERACTIONS IN EARLY CHILDHOOD CLASSROOMS

Early childhood teachers play a very important role in facilitating the development of young children's peer competence (Hamre et al., 2012), especially those with special needs (Kemple, 2004). Unlike parents, classroom teachers have the opportunity to see children within a peer group context on a daily basis, giving them particular insight into children's social behaviors (Kemple, 2004; Recchia & Soucacou, 2006). A teacher's presence and support have been shown to help foster interactions between children with developmental delays and their typically developing peers in inclusive classrooms (Hestenes & Carroll, 2000). Research tells us that frequently teachers must take the initiative to engage children with developmental delays in social interactions and get them involved in nonsolitary play (Harper & McCluskey, 2002). It is important for teachers to consider different ways of supporting relationships among peers in early childhood inclusion classrooms, as these relationships play a critical role in building a classroom community and are essential to children's social development (Guralnick, 2010).

Although a significant number of research studies have focused on the importance of teacher-child relationships in early childhood general education classrooms, there is a surprisingly small number of studies that address this topic for children with special needs (Recchia & Soucacou, 2006). Most researchers have focused on describing specific strategies that teachers can implement in order to foster socially appropriate behaviors in children with disabilities. For example, Batchelor and Taylor (2005) introduced friendship activity interventions, incidental teaching of social skills, and peer-mediated interventions. Friedlander (2009) listed several strategies such as how to structure the physical environment and classroom schedules when children with autism are integrated in a classroom. Both studies also suggest that typically developing peers with developmentally appropriate social skills be encouraged by teachers to teach socially appropriate behaviors to children with disabilities.

Most intervention strategies that are available to teachers are based on developmentally and individually appropriate practices and scientific research. However, many of these strategies seem prescribed and linear; they do not consider the complex nature of social dynamics among children, and the ways in which other aspects of the classroom context can influence children's interactions with peers. Many of the research studies from which recommendations emerge have not explored what teachers need to do in order to implement these strategies, nor examined the ways in which teachers' perceptions of individual children and perspectives on inclusion are closely connected to their behaviors and strategies (Wen, Elicker, & McMullen, 2011).

Thus far, research has not given us any definitive answers regarding how to build an inclusive community among children with diverse learning needs and different personalities (Kemple, 2004). In a recent review of research on peer social competence, Guralnick (2010) concluded that many social skills interventions produce only surface results that young children with disabilities do not generalize beyond the context within which they were learned. Furthermore, there is little evidence that general early childhood practitioners actually integrate these strategies into their teaching on a regular basis (Brown

& Conroy, 2011). Scholars in the field have called for professional development that targets teacher beliefs as a necessary preliminary step to changing teachers' practice (Hamre et al., 2012; Wen et al., 2011).

Unlike the traditional and more strategy-focused interventions for supporting peer interactions suggested in much of the literature, in this chapter we address teacher competencies, emphasizing how teachers' ways of thinking about teaching and learning can have a significant impact on their ways of encouraging socialization among children and building a social community in their classrooms. Scholars who endorse a Disability Studies in Education (DSE) philosophy emphasize the essential connection between how teachers view children with special needs and how responsive they are to inclusion. According to Valle and Connor (2011), the way that a teacher conceptualizes students with disabilities has everything to do with their educational outcomes. In his suggestions for teachers, for example, Connor (2011) discusses the importance of seeing children as individuals first, regardless of labels; listening to students; and watching how they learn.

In order to explain how teacher competencies are developed and translated into practice, we begin by discussing the critical role of reflection in teaching. Teacher reflection has been advocated by many researchers and scholars (Dewey, 1998/1933; Kagan, 1992; Pedro, 2006; Recchia, Beck, Esposito, & Tarrant, 2009; Rodgers, 2002) as the first step in transforming teachers' practice. In this chapter, we articulate a process through which teachers can begin to change their thinking, extend their focus, and start to take action that will make a difference for the young children in their classrooms.

A RECONCEPTUALIZATION OF EARLY CHILDHOOD INCLUSIVE TEACHING

To create truly inclusive early childhood environments, teachers must challenge what they believe they already know, defying theoretical understandings and comfortable ways of being to see what's missing and to create new ways of knowing (Elliot, 2010). As Lubeck (1991) so poignantly stated:

> To reconceptualize . . . is to question what we do, why we do it, whose interests are served, and what the consequences are, both intended and unintended. And, tentatively, in pale and halting strokes, to reconceptualize is also to begin to fill in what is missing and what could be. To reconceptualize is to be angry and to dream. (p. 168)

This way of changing thinking to change action when applied to early childhood inclusion asks teachers to interrupt the usual and customary discourse so that children can engage in shared learning across boundaries of difference. It asks teachers to rethink some of what they have previously learned and experienced as they change their practices to proactively support reciprocal empowerment for children with and without labels. These new ways of knowing are informed by teachers' and caregivers' intuitive and emotional understandings of diverse young children which are not always guided by theory or previous research. Furthermore, what we learn in practice does not always validate theory, as practice moves faster than theory (Adair, 2011), and in fact, practice may lead theory (Williams, 1996).

The first step toward rethinking inclusive practice in early childhood classrooms is to revisit the role of teachers as reflective practitioners. Research tells us that most teachers come to their practice with notions of teaching and learning that are based on their own experiences at school and in the world (Kagan, 1992; Lortie, 1975). For most of these new teachers, current ideas about inclusive classrooms are new. Early childhood classroom environments today are becoming increasingly diverse, which in turn places demands on teachers to think differently about building classroom communities. Changing perceptions to cultivate new competencies often begins with reflection, which serves as a central component in the process of transformative learning, and is increasingly recognized as an essential characteristic of quality educators (Pedro, 2006). Critical reflection is stimulated when teachers encounter practices, environments, and people that do not mirror their expectations and preconceived ideas of teaching and learning (Kaufman, 1996). According to Dewey (1998/1933), "As long as our activity glides smoothly from one thing to another . . . there is no need for reflection" (p. 14). Rather, it is the disorienting event or dilemma, or the culmination of disorientating experiences over time, that fosters reflection and transformative learning (Cranton, 2006; Mezirow, 1997).

Reflective thinking has been described in the literature as different from other kinds of thinking. When teachers reflect, they are thinking to learn. Looked at in this way, reflection becomes a process that leads to deeper understandings of issues, creating meaning from experience. According to Rodgers (2002), attitudes and dispositions are a part of reflective thinking, as the process includes open-mindedness toward discovery and a responsibility to act on what you discover. As such, the reflective process is a necessary component of reconceptulizing practice.

Reflection has also been considered as a way of taking perspective in the context of professionalism (Heffron, Ivins, & Weston, 2005). When teachers reflect, they must get in touch with their own internal reactions to situations as they consider alternative responses. Heffron et al. (2005) discuss the ways that reflective practice contributes to self-awareness and attunement in teachers' work with children and families. Both Heffron et al. (2005) and Rodgers (2002) endorse reflection as a collaborative process that is not fully complete without interaction with others. Only in expressing your thoughts to others can you reveal both the strengths and the holes in your thinking (Rodgers, 2002). Engaging in reflection contributes to quality teaching as "teachers teach best what they understand deeply from their own experience" (Rodgers, 2002, p. 864).

When teachers encounter practical dilemmas in their teaching of particular children, or are faced with young children's challenging behaviors in their classrooms, it is often easy at first to see these issues as the children's problems. Children who respond in a different or unexpected way are viewed as not "fitting in" or as having needs that are too challenging to accommodate. Traditional views of young children with special needs reflect this deficit perspective (Guralnick, 2010). In this chapter, we want to shift the focus to a view of the classroom as a setting in which powerful group dynamics unfold, which can create experiences of inclusion or exclusion for particular children (Lee & Recchia, 2008). Reflecting on classroom dilemmas through a different lens can create space for teachers to reconsider what is happening and to generate new ways to respond that better promote classroom community. As we discuss the six teacher competencies, we hope to provide a catalyst for helping teachers develop this different way of seeing, through which it becomes increasingly clear that establishing a truly inclusive environment requires the ability to see differences as an asset rather than an obstacle.

THE SIX TEACHER COMPETENCIES
FOR AN INCLUSIVE CLASSROOM

In this section we describe six essential teacher competencies that we believe, when enacted in practice, can make a meaningful difference in the social experiences of young children in inclusive early childhood classrooms. They take time and practice to develop, and most teachers will not always be able to enact them in all situations. Embedded within each is a dispositional orientation that fosters a sense of openness, a stance of inquiry, and a holistic understanding of equity.

Teacher dispositions speak to the values, beliefs, and commitments that teachers hold dear on a personal and professional level. They have been described by Carroll (2005) as the link between teachers' knowledge and beliefs and their behavior, particularly regarding the social and moral qualities of their actions. Dispositions become clear in the ways that teachers engage in professional decision making in all aspects of their practice.

Kemple (2004) describes effective inclusion teachers as those who "view teaching as a continual problem-solving process" (p. 20). They have the ability to make connections between their observations of children within the classroom context and their own practice as teachers. In taking an inquiry stance, they think through classroom dilemmas and are willing to try out multiple solutions. She discusses this process as a reflective teaching cycle that teachers engage in as a regular part of their practice.

In thinking about creating an inclusive community, early childhood teachers must also consider how their dispositions can affect the emotional climate in their classrooms. Kemple (2004) describes the ways that a positive emotional atmosphere can set the tone for inclusion by giving children the following messages: "This is a place you can trust"; "this is a caring place"; and "you belong here" (p. 49). This kind of emotional support has been closely linked to children's social development, and there is some evidence that emotionally supportive teaching and positive teacher-student relationships also have an impact on children's academic learning (Hamre et al., 2012).

As we revisit examples from the previous two chapters, we discuss how teachers' responses need to be rooted in deeper understandings of children with special needs and in careful observations of children within the context of their lives and their social relationships within the early childhood classroom and beyond. Rather than simply responding to each situation as it arises, we suggest that teachers must think deeply about their own beliefs and their long-range goals for the young children they are teaching as they find strategies and practices that can make a difference in how the children in their classrooms will come to understand their social world. Although our examples from real early childhood classrooms and our suggested alternative scenarios will not apply directly to every classroom, we hope that they will help teachers generate their own new ideas that can be applied within their own classroom contexts.

Competency 1. Ways of Thinking/Ways of Being That Embrace Difference and Capitalize on Opportunities to Bring Children Together

This competency speaks to the ways that teachers need to work collaboratively with children so that every child becomes a contributor. Early childhood teachers have the opportunity to bring each child's ideas into the group, making other children aware of what their peers have to offer. This can be accomplished by creating multiple moments throughout the day beyond whole-group meetings, which allow all children's voices to be heard.

Early childhood teachers often have their own visions of appropriate ways for children to voice their ideas, particularly within a group setting. For example, a common expectation is for children to raise their hands during circle time and state their comments clearly, in order to have them "count" as contributions to the group. To what extent are teachers privileging certain competencies through these expectations? This everyday activity allows children who are highly verbal and thrive in group-sharing contexts to repeatedly display their competence. Those children who are less comfortable contributing in a large group have fewer opportunities to make their knowledge visible to their peers.

Thinking back to our discussion of Abigail in Chapter 3, we see that her greatest strength was her physical ability, which she could demonstrate most readily in the gym. Within the classroom, however, particularly within a large group, she had few opportunities to display her intellectual voice, leaving other children with no idea what she was thinking and little opportunity to see her as a child with a good idea. Abigail did not demand teachers' attention in the ways that some other children did and could easily be lost on the periphery when things got hectic, as shown in the anecdotal examples in Chapter 3.

What could Abigail's teachers do to make a greater difference in her experience as a fully included member of the group? How could they respond differently to Abigail to make her more visible to her peers? One possibility, as suggested in Chapter 3, might be to provide more opportunities for all of the children to have an option to respond in nonverbal or more active ways within the classroom. This would give both Abigail and other quieter children a new avenue for being active group members, and bring greater value to diverse strengths and capacities in all of the children.

In order to do this, teachers need to implement differentiated instruction within multiple social and learning situations within their classrooms. Giving children diverse ways of showing who they are as members of the community allows individuals to reveal more parts of themselves to the group. For example, some children tend to be more vibrant during physical activities while others are more comfortable expressing their opinions verbally; some children like to take charge of social situations while others prefer to be a good follower or participant rather than a leader. A thriving community needs all kinds of members to contribute to its success. How a teacher values, makes decisions about, and reinforces what "counts" as a meaningful response within the classroom sends a strong message to the children about what and who will be valued in their classrooms.

In our discussion of Joey in Chapter 2, we see how his teacher repeats what he says at group time because he tends to speak softly and to slur his words together. In doing this, she gives Joey a voice and makes sure that it is heard by others. Both Abigail's and Joey's teachers are positioned to make a difference by creating opportunities for the children to fully participate in the group. Furthermore, in taking these kinds of actions, the teachers also bring into others' awareness the children's ideas and capacities, and actively demonstrate ways to accommodate their differences.

In creating a socially inclusive classroom, teachers need to see themselves as the hub through which all the children can become connected. This competency is rooted in DSE ideology, where marginalization is viewed as a function of a social system, as opposed to an individual's differences (Kliewer & Biklen, 2007; Valle & Connor, 2011). Both Joey and Abigail might traditionally be seen as children who would benefit most from initiating language, and the typical strategies for encouraging language would emphasize elaborating on their spontaneous utterances (Stanton-Chapman & Hadden, 2011). The strategies discussed here, however, go beyond explicit word production skills, and encourage making space for new understandings of potential teaching and learning relationships that embrace reciprocal shared knowledge, emotional connectedness, and community consciousness for diverse young children. When teachers start out by asking how they can bring the group together, this thinking guides their changes in action.

The following questions provide a catalyst for reflecting on your practice in relation to this competency. Remember, changes in thinking bring you one step closer toward changes in action.

- To what extent am I open to children's different ways of expressing their opinions?
- When I make a decision based on children's input, who are the key players? How wide is the circle of children who influence my decision?

Competency 2. The Capacity to Nurture and Embrace Each Child as a Unique Individual Who Brings a Special Contribution to the Group

Teachers demonstrate this competency as they further illuminate children's individual strengths for others in the group by creating special opportunities for different children's contributions to be recognized and valued. Figuratively, teachers' behaviors and responses are like a mirror through which children's small successes are reflected back to others in the group. In order to develop this competency, teachers must view children through a strengths-based perspective, as articulated in DSE ideology (Kliewer & Biklen, 2007). For example, in Abigail's case, the recommendation for practice centers on creating multiple opportunities throughout the day for different children's voices to be heard. The next critical step is how teachers respond to comments/input from children like Abigail, who tend to get lost in the group, helping to make their ideas and behaviors accessible and valuable to others.

How do teachers create and capitalize on opportunities for children to be contributors with something to say that others want to hear? What if Abigail's teachers talked about the things that happen in the gym at group time, emphasizing activities that she excels at? Would she be more motivated to participate actively in the discussion? What if there were opportunities to communicate nonverbally, acting out ideas rather than always stating them orally? Would Abigail be more willing to enter into this different kind of dialogue?

Looking back at Ira in Chapter 3, what could his teacher have done to highlight his strengths in the anecdotal situations described? How could she have better helped Calvin to see Ira's special contribution? Ira so wants to capture Calvin's attention, but is struggling to find a way to be valued by him. By allowing Calvin to ignore Ira, does his teacher inadvertently give the message that this is acceptable behavior? Does she pass up an opportunity to encourage Calvin to be accountable for his rejection of Ira? Could she help Calvin see Ira in a different light?

In order to make individual children's strengths and special contributions visible to the group, teachers must first get to know the children they are teaching as the unique individuals they are. Ira, in this case, is very motivated to follow Calvin's lead in play. He is aware enough to have discovered that Calvin enjoys "potty talk" and tries to use his own version of it to gain Calvin's attention. Although his teacher may not want to reinforce this choice of interaction, could she capitalize on Ira's interest in following Calvin's lead in another way? In the heat of an emotional interaction it may be difficult to gain Calvin's immediate cooperation, but being aware of Ira's interest in making a connection with Calvin might guide the teacher to take action at other times to bring the boys together.

For teachers to develop this competency, the first step is to acknowledge their own biases toward individual children. In Ira's case, for example, the teacher may have her own negative perceptions of Ira and his role in the classroom. She would need to reflect on her own feelings about him and his capacity to be Calvin's, as well as other children's, friend. It will be difficult for her to encourage other children to be Ira's friend if she does not value what he brings to the group. Self-awareness is the first step in the process as teachers move toward changing their own perspectives on particular children whom they may be viewing through a deficit lens.

The following questions provide a catalyst for reflecting on your practice in relation to this competency. Remember, changes in thinking bring you one step closer toward changes in action.

- Can I identify the individual strengths of all of the children in my classroom? Is there any child for whom I am having trouble doing this?
- How often do I articulate each child's strength to other children throughout the day?

Competency 3. Openness to Reconsidering, Rethinking, and Redoing Teaching and Learning Activities with Children in Response to Their Input

Too often special education teachers are overly focused on the specific outcomes (skills) that children with special needs attain from an activity (e.g., how long a child plays with a peer). To truly include children in daily classroom experience, teachers need to rethink what makes an activity valuable to each child, and redo activities in response to children's input. Consider Adam from Chapter 2, the boy with physical challenges who needed assistance to be a full participant in play.

Once Adam got the chair close to the table, he needed assistance to get into it. Jenny, his teacher, continued to facilitate Adam's assisted independence. In this example, Jenny's goal was to provide physical assistance for Adam so that he could engage with the other children.

We posed the question: What might have happened if Jenny thought more about ways of incorporating the process of Adam's transition itself into a classroom activity with peers? Maybe it is more important to acknowledge and affirm Adam's motivation to move independently than to assist him to participate in ways that take this freedom away from him. Could Jenny have shifted her expectations so that she could honor Adam's experience instead of imposing her own goal? In order to do this, Jenny would have to go with the process in the moment, and be less concerned with the immediate outcome. She would have to give up some control, as this new way of teaching would include not only teacher-generated activities designed to promote children's learning in the group, but also an openness to incorporating differentiated responses to meet children's individual needs.

Now let's consider Mario and his interaction with his friend Jane, also discussed in Chapter 2. Mario's teacher enters their sandbox interaction by taking the perspective of Jane, who by traditional developmental standards would be considered a more cognitively competent peer. Jane is engaging in a lesson around measurement which is very creative. She tries to engage Mario in the lesson but he shows no interest. Instead, he prefers to explore the sand on a sensory level. What might have happened if the teacher shifted her expectation so that she could create an activity that honored Mario's experience as well as Jane's point of view? Might the activity have taken a new direction?

One possibility would have been to take a more process-oriented stance as opposed to focusing directly on the learning outcome. Research on young children's capacity for learning through spontaneous play experiences supports early childhood teaching and learning in play-based and process-oriented contexts (Bergen, 2009; Bodrova, 2008). By attending to Mario's expressed interests, his teacher could capitalize on his motivation and engagement in this sensory activity, perhaps even enticing Jane toward more sensory exploration. When teachers consider children's emotions, motivations, and engagement as essential elements of learning, and express a willingness to go with the process, be in the moment, and take cues from the child, they are able to create opportunities that allow diverse children to be integrated in every part of classroom experience.

The approach that we are encouraging through this competency requires that teachers be willing to think "outside the box" of traditional and prevalent early childhood and special education practices.

To create truly inclusive early childhood environments, teachers must challenge what they may have learned in the past and perhaps their own previous beliefs about teaching, learning, and the potential value of what diverse children have to offer to the curriculum. Changing the ways they teach may be difficult at first, as they will have to give up their old agendas to embrace new ways of knowing, informed by their intuitive and emotional understandings of diverse young children. To develop this competency, teachers must be open to being surprised by the unexpected abilities and understandings that children may bring to the classroom, and also be ready to think creatively about multiple ways to support diverse learning styles.

The following questions provide a catalyst for reflecting on your practice in relation to this competency. Remember, changes in thinking bring you one step closer toward changes in action.

- How comfortable am I when my lesson plan has to be changed or my planned activity is interrupted because children are more motivated to do something else?
- When a child offers a different way to approach a task or solve a problem, how often do I make space in my teaching plan to highlight that child's contribution?
- When I am working with a small or large group of children, how do I differentiate so that children with different abilities and learning styles can fully engage in the activity?

Competency 4. The Ability to Attend to the Child's Perspective When Making Decisions That Impact Daily Experiences

In order for teachers to take a child's perspective, they need to be conscious of how they position themselves, classroom activities, and other children, so that the child can be an active participant in the activity. Teachers need to focus more on what children are learning from the situation and less on controlling children's behavior, as they adapt their approaches and make accommodations to support individual learners. DSE ideology supports teachers as advocates for children's rights, who are able to see disabilities as differences, not deficits (Valle & Connor, 2011).

Looking back at Adam in Chapter 2, we see an example of how the teaching and learning perspective can change when the teacher starts by being attuned to what is most motivating for the child. Adam is highly motivated to move independently, but allowing him to do this may take away from his time to participate in some planned classroom activities. Adam's physical needs and challenges get in the way of his easy access to the curriculum that Jenny has planned. We posed the question: What can she do differently to honor Adam's desire to practice independent movement while still supporting his engagement in group activities?

In working with a child with physical disabilities, teachers need to make a special effort to adapt their own physical presence (e.g., the way they sit in relation to the children) and that of other children in the group. Teachers need to plan activities based on the children's motivation and interests, building on their knowledge of how each child actively engages in classroom experiences and what each child is likely to gain from the activity.

Reflecting back on Joey's story in Chapter 2, we see how his teacher, Kathy, is able to make decisions based on seeing situations through Joey's eyes. She knows, for example, that he especially likes to sit in the "big chair" at meeting time, and that indulging this desire creates a more comfortable space for him that allows him to participate more fully in the group activities. Kathy does not see this decision as a way of giving Joey special treatment or reinforcing his bad habits, but rather as a way of supporting his particular needs as a group participant. She takes the view that Joey's comfort is good for the group, as his engagement in the ongoing activity enriches the overall experience for everyone.

Sometimes it is difficult at first for a teacher to understand why an individual child might have a particular interest or desire. Traditional suggestions for responding to behavioral differences like these tend to operate from a deficit perspective, with a goal of "normalizing" children's behavior. What Kathy does instead validates Joey's preferences, honoring his choices and letting others know that individual choices are valued in this classroom. When children demonstrate idiosyncratic or unusual expressions in their social behaviors, teachers can make a difference by respecting the child's point of view and designing curricular experiences based on what will bring the best response from an individual child.

This competency may seem like a given for many early childhood teachers, who are so often experts at taking a child's point of view. However, in the midst of a bustling early childhood classroom, it is easy to get caught up in the rules and structures that help manage the flow of activity. Sometimes the established rules and routines have to be reconsidered, however, in the best interest of an individual child. We are asking teachers to consider the ways that small changes can make a big difference in children's experiences as integral members of the classroom community.

The following questions provide a catalyst for reflecting on your practice in relation to this competency. Remember, changes in thinking bring you one step closer toward changes in action.

- How often do I think about/imagine how children may feel in a certain situation or in response to an activity that I present? Am I able to put myself in each child's shoes, or is it easier to take the perspective of some but not others?
- Am I willing to make changes in the regular routines of the day to accommodate a particular child's differences? Do I incorporate the child's perspective into my decision making?

Competency 5. The Expectation That All Children Can Meet Appropriate Educational and Developmental Goals and a Willingness to Support Their Efforts; a Belief That Children Can and Will Be Successful

When considering the elements of successful inclusive practice in classrooms, most teachers express concerns about children's challenging behaviors (Dunlap & Fox, 2011). Teachers assume that children's behavior must be under control before they can meaningfully participate in classroom activities. Even when teachers see children's strengths, they don't always know how to capitalize on them, particularly in the face of challenging behavior. Instead of focusing so much on negative behaviors, teachers need to shift their thinking from controlling behaviors to creating opportunities for success. DSE ideology articulates inclusion as a state of mind that translates to action (Valle & Connor, 2011).

Looking back at Cody's story in Chapter 3, we see how his teacher, Camille, did not give up on him. She kept trying to come up with new strategies to accommodate his challenging emotional outbursts, giving him the message that his dangerous behaviors would not be tolerated but there were other, more appropriate ways that he could be a member of the group. Cody's behavior could be overwhelming, and Camille needed to protect the other children. She came up with a unique strategy, taking the group, instead of Cody, out of the classroom. Although this strategy could be disruptive to the group, it allowed Camille to stop reinforcing Cody's provocative, attention-seeking behavior while also giving him the message that interesting group activities were waiting just outside the door once he was able to calm down and rejoin the group.

In a sense, Camille's use of this strategy allowed her to capitalize on Cody's social strengths because she knew that he was very motivated to be with his peers. Camille shows how teachers can move beyond simply controlling negative behaviors in disruptive children. The first practical step is to observe children's moments of success, and to create opportunities to increase them. Teachers can't ignore a child who throws a chair toward his peers, but they can pay more attention when he is showing positive and socially appropriate behaviors.

Now consider Ira's story in Chapter 3. What would have happened if his teacher, Beverly, responded differently to his frustration over being ignored by Calvin? Instead of telling him to find another friend, she could have reminded him of the moments when he was successful at getting children's attention. Even though it might not be possible to enact a positive turnaround in that moment, by helping Ira to reengage with his own memories of previous positive social experiences, Beverly would be expressing her belief in his ability to be successful. Saying something like "Calvin is not listening to you right now, but I remember that yesterday you were playing together with the blocks and you seemed to be having a lot of fun" could help Ira reengage his memory of a positive social experience, and perhaps even change his outlook.

Early childhood teachers are uniquely positioned as advocates for young children as they have the power to help children see their own strengths on a daily basis. By calling into focus images of positive accomplishments teachers can help children who are struggling with social situations to highlight moments of success rather than dwell on negative experiences. By expressing their beliefs in young children's abilities to be successful, teachers can make a difference in how children come to see themselves as members of the classroom community.

This competency speaks to the need for teachers to look beyond the labels that children are assigned, all of which can be exclusionary, to see and believe in the strengths within each individual. Certain labels, such as "emotion regulation disorder", automatically place children under scrutiny. As advocates for children, early childhood teachers are uniquely situated to support children's early learning success, which is foundational to all later learning. Teachers who are able to see the children they teach as more than the "troublemaker," "class clown," "tyrant," "bully," or even the "kid who doesn't get it," can help children work from their own strengths. Envisioning new possibilities for them, teachers can make all the difference in their lives.

The following questions provide a catalyst for reflecting on your practice in relation to this competency. Remember, changes in thinking bring you one step closer toward changes in action.

- When do I give up on children because I assume that they can't do certain things? When thinking about these children, do I remember moments of their success?
- Do I continue to think creatively and keep trying new strategies to support children's success when initial strategies fail?

Competency 6. An Understanding That "Equity" Does Not Always Mean "Equality" in an Inclusive Environment; Because Different People Need Different Things to Have "Equal" Access, Treating Children Differently Is Acceptable

Viewing all communications as meaningful social attempts that can be built on in the classroom opens up the possibility to reconceptualize children's behaviors in new and more positive ways and to tailor responses to support social success. Starting with the belief that all behaviors are communicative, teachers need to figure out what children are trying to tell them, and how to give children the most powerful message in return. Not all children need the same things at the same time, nor will they all optimally respond to the same set of rules or expectations. DSE ideology supports strengths-based perspectives that consider disabilities as diversities and difference as the norm (Danforth, 2006).

Looking back at Cody's story in Chapter 3, we see how his teacher, Camille, works tirelessly to find a way to break through his negative social behaviors. Although Camille does not use the same techniques with other children in the classroom, she has carefully considered and adapted a strategy that seems to be working for Cody. Cody's negative behavior often starts with a little thing which annoys somebody, and then gets out of control really fast. Being out of control in a big way requires a special response, especially when other children's safety is at risk. Camille has already tried more customary strategies such as using time-out within the classroom and has not been satisfied with the results. She thinks "outside the box" to find a way to match her responses to Cody's way of thinking. In Cody's case, isolation ends up being a very powerful incentive to get his behavior under control. Even though his behavior might have sometimes appeared antisocial on the outside, what he really wanted on the inside was to be a part of the group. Taking away that opportunity was the most effective way to control his behavior.

Reflecting on Joey's story in Chapter 2, we see how his teacher, Kathy, gives him the message and also sends the message to the other children that it is acceptable for one child to have some special experiences in the classroom—everyone does not have to be the same. When she allows Joey to sit on the special chair for meeting time, she demonstrates that individual differences are valued in her classroom. Although some teachers might see Kathy's approach as showing favoritism or reinforcing a child's obsessive behavior, we argue that she is taking a more holistic view of how to best support Joey to be an active and engaged member of the classroom community. She has observed that sitting on the big chair has an impact on his ability to relax and increases his participation in the group meeting time. When Joey is calm and engaged, the meeting goes better for everyone.

Questions of fairness are a great concern for many early childhood teachers (Lee & Recchia, 2008; Mullarkey, Recchia, Lee, Lee, & Shin, 2005). So many challenging situations arise when working with a group of small children who must share both the material and interpersonal resources in the classroom. However, not all children want or need the same kinds of resources to do well within the group. Moreover, some children have particular needs that can only be addressed adequately with additional teacher support. When there are too many rules about fairness in the classroom, teachers can inadvertently miss opportunities to support children's social experiences (Kluth & Schwartz, 2008; Recchia & Soucacou, 2006).

Consider, for example, a child who takes a cracker from his peer at snack time. Is this always wrong or unfair? What if the "thief" typically does not initiate social interactions with peers? Viewing this act as a meaningful social attempt to make a connection with a peer, which can then be built on in the classroom, opens up the possibility to conceptualize that child's behavior in new and more positive ways. How a teacher responds to situations like these can make all the difference in how children experience each other within the classroom community. If she recites a rule like "No touching other people's food!" she gives the message that the child in question is misbehaving, but if she chooses to respond by saying, "Are you asking your friend for a cracker?" she opens up the possibility for a positive social interaction. Her response reflects back to the individual child, as well as to the peer, possibilities not only for how this behavior will be interpreted, but for how the child taking the cracker will be seen by others. If she characterizes the child taking the cracker as behaving badly, she helps to establish this role for him. But if she sees the behavior as an emergent social strength in a child with special needs and an opportunity for a meaningful interaction between peers, she might give a very different message.

This competency asks teachers to rethink their own concepts of fairness and equity in their work with young children and to consider new possibilities for teaching and learning in their classrooms. It also requires that teachers be open to seeing beyond the behaviors that children present today, to support their growth toward positive change tomorrow. It is easy to be tempted to close the door of an "inclusive" classroom to children who are aggressive and/or can potentially hurt others, or who will have difficulty at first "fitting in." It is challenging and can be uncomfortable for teachers to come to terms with their own fears or expectations that aggressive or antisocial children will not be able to participate in building a safe and supportive classroom community. Children like Cody are often excluded from inclusive classrooms and placed in a segregated classroom with others who have similar behavioral issues, before being given the chance to succeed with peers who engage in more socially appropriate interactions. Teachers need to believe in children like Cody and look beyond his behaviors. Although it might have been much easier for Camille to manage her classroom without him being a member, she was able to see Cody's potential and was motivated to help him find his own strengths. In order to act on this competency, teachers must become comfortable with considering alternative, sometimes controversial, teaching strategies in the short term, as an investment in potentially greater and more long-term effects on children's future experiences as members of an inclusive community.

The following questions provide a catalyst for reflecting on your practice in relation to this competency. Remember, changes in thinking bring you one step closer toward changes in action.

- How do I define fairness? How do I enact my beliefs about fairness in my daily practice?
- What kinds of changes to usual and customary practices am I willing to make to accommodate particular needs of individual children?

TEACHER COMPETENCIES AS A FRAMEWORK FOR TRANSFORMING TEACHING AND LEARNING IN THE EARLY CHILDHOOD CLASSROOM

The six teacher competencies discussed above speak to a growing need within educational settings to move beyond narrow conceptions of ability and disability to take a transformative stance that supports diversity and community for all learners. With a focus on diversity as the norm, a space is created for reconceptualizing meanings and practices of social inclusion. Our focus on everyday classroom practices demonstrates the ways that competent teachers' small steps in the classroom can bring big ideas, both theoretical and ideological, to life in everyday practice.

These competencies provide a framework for teachers as they begin to engage in new ways of conceptualizing their classroom practices that move beyond simple, *directive* statements about "globally effective" strategies found in the literature, to a process-oriented and dynamic approach to transforming practice through everyday actions. Looking holistically at teacher competencies through a DSE lens allows us to move beyond simple statements of what to do, leading to clearer explanations for weaving together theory and teacher beliefs and practices.

The teachers in our stories are from diverse classrooms where everyday dilemmas of practice must be addressed in the moment. Although it is not always possible to enact each teacher competency described above, we hope that the stories and suggestions provide a vision for readers of not only what is possible under the best of circumstances, but of strategies and practices they can imagine enacting in their own classrooms with their own students. In order to help you begin this process, we present Table 4.1, which synthesizes the changes in thinking that each competency addresses and the changes in action that follow.

Developing these teacher competencies as a part of teaching practice is a process that takes time, ongoing reflection, and a commitment to taking action. Each school and classroom is different, and there is not a "one size fits all" model that can address everyone's needs adequately. Enacting inclusive practice requires a flexible and accommodating stance, and a belief that all children can grow and learn within your classroom community.

Developing teacher competencies is not a linear process. Working with young children is ongoing and dynamic, and changes in practice take time and patience. These six competencies, although described individually for clarity of communication, are often integrated in teachers' responses to children. Reflection pushes teachers to think deeply not only about their own actions, but also about the responses they receive from children. As teachers change their thinking and refine their actions, they will see the impact of this process in children's social experiences as members of the classroom community.

TABLE 4.1. Applying Competencies to Practice

Competency	Change in Thinking (Questions that encourage teachers to examine their thought processes)	Change in Action (Questions that encourage teachers to change their behaviors)
1. Ways of thinking/ways of being that embrace difference and capitalize on opportunities to bring children together	To what extent am I open to children's different ways of expressing their opinions?	What do I do when I notice that children are not participating? How can I include more children in group discussions?
2. Capacity to nurture and embrace each child as a unique individual who brings a special contribution to the group	Can I identify the individual strengths of all of the children in my classroom? Is there any child for whom I am having trouble doing this?	What do I do to help children appreciate the individual strengths of their peers?
3. Openness to reconsidering, rethinking, and redoing teaching and learning activities with children in response to their input	How comfortable am I when my lesson plan has to be changed or my planned activity is interrupted because children are more motivated to do something else?	What is my initial response to children's expression of their own ideas? How often do I change my own agenda in response to them?
4. The ability to attend to the child's perspective when making decisions that impact daily experiences	How often do I think about/imagine how children may feel in a certain situation or in response to an activity that I present? Am I able to put myself in all of the children's shoes, or is it easier to take the perspective of some versus others?	What do I do to let children know that I understand their feelings? How do I help them represent their feelings to the group?
5. The expectation that all children can meet appropriate educational and developmental goals and a willingness to support their efforts; a belief that children can and will be successful	When do I give up on children because I assume that they can't do certain things? When thinking about these children, do I remember moments of their success?	What efforts do I make to think "outside the box" for children whom I find most challenging?
6. An understanding that "equity" does not always mean "equality" in an inclusive environment; because different people need different things to have "equal" access, treating children differently is acceptable	How do I define "fairness"?	What's my response when children say "it's not fair"? What can I say to children when explaining that fairness is not "getting the same thing," but rather "equally providing what is necessary to each of them"?

The benefits to developing and enacting these teacher competencies go well beyond the classroom. When young children experience difference as an asset rather than a liability, they come to see the world in new ways. As Rogoff (2003) suggests,

> variations among members of communities are to be expected, because individuals connect in various ways with other communities and experiences . . . variation is a resource for humanity, allowing us to be prepared for varied and unknowable futures. (p. 12)

CHAPTER 5

Early Childhood Classrooms as Inclusive Learning Communities

Our Visions for the Future

T HE EARLY CHILDHOOD classroom has become a second home to increasing numbers of young children who spend a good part of their early lives with their teachers and peers. It is within these diverse classrooms that many children have their first experiences in the larger social world, learn what it means to be a part of a classroom community, and develop understandings about themselves and others that are foundational to their ongoing social experiences throughout their lives (Guralnik, 2010; Howes & Ritchie, 2002). Recommended practices in early childhood education endorse teaching and learning opportunities that support the development of strong social and emotional foundations, and see young children's motivation to learn as deeply embedded in their early social and emotional experiences (Grisham-Brown, Hemmeter, & Pretti-Frontczak, 2005). In the context of early relationships, children begin to learn what and who is valued in the social world, and to develop their earliest understandings of their own place within the larger social communities to which they belong.

As we bring together our visions for the future of inclusive early childhood classrooms, we draw on the ideas presented in the previous chapters. We have described a set of classroom components and teacher competencies that we believe can serve as a framework for reconceptualizing early childhood classrooms as inclusive learning communities that serve a wide range of children with and without disability labels, provide access to an authentic and meaningful curriculum for all kinds of learners, and engender deeper understandings of the powerful impact of how teachers teach on what children learn.

In this chapter we articulate the ways that the components and competencies come together within the context of developing relationships in classrooms and schools in everyday practice, and synthesize them within a larger, overarching framework that provides "big ideas" about inclusion. We present three overarching principles for inclusive early childhood practice that serve to ground the components and competencies as they are enacted through a relationship lens. We discuss the ways that our ideas about inclusion can be embedded in the early childhood curriculum, and we explore the kinds of support that is needed to create sustainable changes in the field that go beyond the early childhood classroom.

SYNTHESIZING THE COMPONENTS AND COMPETENCIES THROUGH A RELATIONSHIP LENS

In the previous three chapters we described a series of classroom components and teacher competencies that we applied to particular stories of individual children in different early childhood classrooms. However, our vision of how these components and competencies can guide different teachers' practice allows for their flexible generalization across diverse contexts. Rather than discrete elements to be applied individually and in specific situations, the components and competencies should be viewed as integrated and holistic. We see the components and competencies as overlapping and fully integrated in ways that encourage teachers to envision their own potential transformations in their practice. The framework they provide can support a wide range of inclusive classroom communities.

The significance of relationships as the overarching unifier of the components and competencies, as well as the impetus for their dynamic enactment in classrooms, cannot be underestimated. Inclusive classrooms and schools require attention to relationships at every level of interaction. Meaningful relationships serve as the foundation that holds the components and competencies together, and these relationships also contribute to the ways in which inclusive classrooms can become dynamic, socially responsive environments. When we look through a relationship lens, some questions take on new meaning: How do teachers respond to children? What are their attitudes toward and strategies for working with children with disability labels? How do teachers feel about inclusion? The questions are not simply theoretical or objective, but grounded in teachers' understandings of the real children and families with whom they interact on a daily basis. Early childhood teachers who know well and care deeply about the children in their classrooms will most likely find the relationship lens a natural one, through which they can enact the components and competencies.

The power of relationships extends well beyond the teachers and children within an individual classroom. Relationships with professionals and families are equally important in grounding and sustaining inclusive practices. Shared understandings with coteachers, assistants, families, and administrators create a strong foundation for making fundamental changes in thinking that can lead to meaningful and lasting changes in the action taken to support inclusion in schools and communities.

THE OVERARCHING PRINCIPLES FOR INCLUSIVE PRACTICE

Our vision for the future of early childhood inclusion begins with the enactment of the components and competencies within early childhood classrooms, but extends to a systems level, where enduring changes in inclusive practice can become fully enmeshed in the fabric of school policy. Envisioning how and where the fundamental changes need to take place leads to larger and more far-reaching conceptualizations of inclusion. In stepping back from the individual classroom to reconceptualize inclusion policy, we look more broadly at three overarching principles, or "big ideas," about inclusion that are essential to our framework. They include: inclusion as community; inclusion as a dynamic process; and inclusion as social transformation. Each of these principles is described in greater detail in the following sections.

Principle 1: Inclusion is About Community. It Is More Than a Placement or a Service. It Involves Creating Shared Spaces, Bringing People Together, and Giving Them a Voice.

Traditionally, a setting is called "inclusive" when it serves as a placement for at least one child identified with a disability within a general education setting (Friend & Shamberger, 2008). In this view, inclusion is accomplished when children with special needs are found in the same physical classroom space as their typically developing peers. Looking through a relationship lens to enact the components and competencies presented in this book, we ask teachers and administrators to take one step further toward a conceptualization of inclusive practice that incorporates children's social and emotional experiences as members of a classroom community. Inclusion from this perspective is not just about bringing everyone together in the same space; more important, it is about creating a space within which individuals make meaningful social and emotional connections with each other, and where children have a sense of "belonging, being valued, and having choices" (Horn, Thompson, Palmer, Jenson, & Turbiville, 2004, p. 207).

Articulated in our six classroom components presented in Chapters 2 and 3, this relationship-based way of thinking about inclusion provides a framework for creating early childhood classroom environments that bring all members of the community together (#5), provide support for diverse learners (#3), make curricula accessible in multiple ways (#1), support diversity as the norm (#4), capitalize on children's strengths (#6), and prioritize interpersonal connections (#2). Inclusion through this lens goes beyond the mandates of special education law (Hyatt, 2007) to ensure that children are not merely placed in inclusive settings, but that they have truly inclusive experiences.

Our six classroom components serve as building blocks for creating inclusive classroom communities. To bring inclusion practice to life within the classroom, however, it is essential that teachers make an ongoing commitment to actively engage in the process of inclusive teaching, reflected in the six teacher competencies. The next principle captures the essence of this dynamic process in which teachers play a critical role.

Principle 2: Inclusion Is a Dynamic Process. It Occurs Within a Living Classroom Community That Continually Changes in Response to Its Members, Their Interests, and Their Needs.

The early childhood inclusive classrooms we envision are places where both children and adults are engaged in active learning. Changes in teachers' thinking about what makes their classrooms inclusive can lead to changes in their actions in everyday practice. Children will feel the effects of these changes and adapt their own ways of thinking and being in response to them. This reciprocal and synergistic process of ongoing change, guided by the teacher competencies, fuels the ongoing process of creating more meaningful and authentic social and emotional connections, which are at the core of relationship-based inclusive experience.

Our six teacher competencies presented in Chapter 4 provide a framework to help guide teachers' thinking as they navigate the day-to-day process of bringing inclusion to life in their classrooms. As teachers embrace children's differences (#1), respond to children's unique ideas (#3), demonstrate their belief in children's abilities (#5), take children's perspectives (#4), take a stance of equity over equality (#6), and nurture and appreciate each child (#2), they help to create a growth-oriented classroom environment that is continually shaped and reshaped by the members of the community. Teaching and learning are seen as fluid and flexible entities which find meaning within a dynamic context.

Principle #3: Inclusion is About Social Transformation. Small Changes Can Make a Big Difference Over Time. Changes in Thinking Lead to Changes in Action.

Looking at the classroom components and teacher competencies together, we see a framework to guide inclusive practice that goes beyond each small classroom community. As individual teachers begin to embrace these ideas, bringing their changes in thinking to a place of action, the potential grows for larger and more substantive change that can be scaled up to schools and local communities. Taking your personal experiences with inclusion to the next level through the process of nurturing and challenging others to rethink their own assumptions is a critical step toward transforming others' thinking about the value of building truly inclusive communities. Social transformation comes about when we move beyond our own comfort zones to reach out to others and engage them in the change process.

Global decisions that arise within your school or community can present ongoing opportunities for working toward social transformation. When called on to express your opinion on where to place children who have been labeled as "difficult to manage," or what parameters should be set for classroom groupings at your school, take these events as opportunities to bring your changing ideas about creating inclusive communities to action. Each time a colleague leans toward changing children's behaviors to better fit his or her own expectations, or an administrator considers a new policy that may inadvertently exclude some children, think about ways that you can articulate your new ways of thinking to potentially broaden the mindsets of other members of the community.

These ideas reflect ways of thinking "outside the box," and looking beyond what's happening at the current moment to envision a more inclusive future for children with disabilities. This way of thinking is articulated in the field of Disability Studies in Education (DSE) (Danforth & Gabel, 2006). DSE emphasizes disability as diversity, and views difference through a strength-based perspective. This philo-

sophical orientation promotes inclusion as social change and reinforces the need for more teachers to change their thinking about disability and inclusion. DSE scholars challenge the ideas put forth by
more traditional special education researchers (Gabel, 2005), such as
evidence-based, data-driven strategies for enacting curricula, which
are too often translated to narrow definitions of inclusive practice.
However, although DSE scholars clearly articulate inclusion as social
transformation on a philosophical level, their work often lacks practical suggestions and applications, missing opportunities to apply their
ideas to actual changes in classrooms (Naraian, 2011). The classroom
components and teacher competencies presented here take these philosophical ideas to the next level, offering a framework for moving
changes in thinking toward changes in action within the everyday
classroom environment and beyond.

BRINGING EARLY CHILDHOOD INCLUSION TO LIFE: APPLYING THE CLASSROOM COMPONENTS AND TEACHER COMPETENCIES

Creating inclusive early childhood classrooms that embrace all learners and make a place for everyone at the table may seem at first like a
daunting undertaking, with too many external barriers to overcome.
Changing our own and others' dispositions toward inclusion is a mul-
tistep process that takes time, ongoing reflection, and opportunities to
think about change with the support and collaboration of colleagues,
families, and administrators (Mogharreban & Bruns, 2009; Purcell et al.,
2007). In order to articulate the ways in which our components and
competencies can guide this process, we focus here on three critically
important areas of consideration: creation of a curriculum that reflects
and includes all children, collaboration with professionals and families,
and administrative leadership to create and sustain quality inclusive
practice. Figure 5.1 provides an illustration of the ways in which the
classroom components and the teacher competencies are synthesized
within the context of relationships among community stakeholders.

A Curriculum That Reflects and Includes All Children

Early childhood teachers who embrace diversity and strive to make
meaningful connections with all of the children in their inclusive
classrooms must learn to differentiate instruction to meet the needs
of a wide range of students. Differentiation requires that teachers create

FIGURE 5.1. Synthesis of Classroom Components and Teacher Competentcies

classrooms and curricula that fit students' needs, rather than trying to change their students to fit within the parameters of a particular curriculum. Differentiated instruction has been described in the literature as proactive; more qualitative than quantitative (teaching concepts as opposed to facts); rooted in assessment; student-centered; and a blend of whole-class, group, and individual instruction (Tomlinson, 2001). These dimensions acknowledge student differences, and consider their interests and learning styles as critical components of curriculum design and implementation. However, as we have articulated in the previous chapters, being and feeling included requires more than individualized instruction. Teaching and learning interactions take place within the context of social relationships that nurture and support individual children as valued members of the community. As described in the previous chapters, our vision for inclusive teaching engages a relationship lens as instrumental in guiding decisions in all levels of daily practice.

Teachers who enact an integrated early childhood curriculum in their classrooms in accordance with recommended practices (Cross, Salazar, Dopson-Campuzano, & Batchelder, 2009) know that this multidimensional way of thinking about teaching and learning extends beyond teaching specific skills and knowledge. Rather, young children are viewed as active creators of their own knowledge, as opposed to receptacles for learning. In our vision of the inclusive early childhood classroom, the curriculum is also considered a powerful tool for building relationships with all kinds of children as they actively engage in learning. As teachers develop their curriculum, they must keep in mind the ways in which they are building a foundation not only for future learning, but for children's motivation to learn.

Guided by the classroom components and teacher competencies, the members of the early childhood classroom community create an atmosphere that encourages and supports peer learning and individual growth through their ways of relating to one another. The decisions that teachers make, even in the small moments of classroom instruction, can send powerful messages to individual children and their peers that set the tone for the group. For example, when teachers make the decision to divide children into small groups based on their readiness levels, are they also being conscious of how the children in each group relate to one another socially? What are the advantages of separating children in ways that make evident and reinforce their differences? When teachers convey to the children that individual learning differences are honored in each group, an atmosphere for peer learning and individual growth is fostered. Instead of judging one another's skills, children can be encouraged to acknowledge the ways that everyone learns things differently, and to value these learning differences. When relationships are valued as the foundation for early childhood practice and play a central role in decision making, curricular choices may take shape in new ways.

Collaboration with Professionals and Families

Creating inclusion practices that go beyond a particular classroom, or one highly committed early childhood teacher, requires a vision of community that is shared with others. How teachers collaborate with families and other professionals in this process can set the stage for making changes in classroom- and school-based practices that will become an integral part of children's ongoing school experience, rather than just one lucky year in their lives.

There is an extensive literature in early childhood education and early childhood special education that emphasizes the need for collaboration (Cross et al., 2009; Friend & Shamberger, 2008; Mogharreban & Bruns, 2009). The Division for Early Childhood (DEC) of the Council for Exceptional Children considers interdisciplinary collaboration and family-based practices as critical elements in successfully meeting the needs of young children with disabilities (Cross et al., 2009). The group discusses the importance of developing clearly defined practices for collaborations with families that are individualized, flexible, and strengths-based, and that have been shown through research to have positive outcomes. Its recommendations for professionals include setting expectations for staff, community, and families and providing guidance for service delivery. However, in much of this literature, the focus is on professionals' surface behaviors; less attention is given to the deeper and more authentic experiences around collaboration that are often quite challenging for professionals to achieve. This portrayal of collaboration can lead professionals to make assumptions about the "right" or "appropriate" ways of working with others, ultimately interfering with their ability to adapt their own thinking to accommodate different points of view.

Although these recommendations can offer helpful guidelines for creating successful inclusive services, they do not provide professionals a framework for developing authentic relationships with children, families, and colleagues. The classroom components and teacher competencies described in this book, however, can be used to create such a framework. As teachers develop expertise in the competencies described in Chapter 4, for example, they not only increase their own professional skills, but also demonstrate for children, families, and colleagues a different way of seeing the world. When they take the perspectives of diverse children in their classrooms, and respond to individual differences as elements that enrich the classroom environment, early childhood teachers naturally model a culture of collaboration. This more flexible, open-ended way of thinking about teaching and learning can also extend to more flexible understandings of the perspectives of other adults. As they examine their previous assumptions and develop a more flexible and inclusive mind-set, early childhood teachers will become more able to acknowledge others' points of view. Using a relationship lens to look beyond the children in their classrooms to families and colleagues can help teachers extend their collaborative skills to their work with other adults.

Administrative Leadership That Builds and Sustains Quality Inclusive Practice

What kinds of support do teachers need to effectively enact the classroom components and teacher competencies that we have talked about in this book? How can administrators and supervisors at their sites make a difference in the everyday experiences of young children in inclusive classrooms? How does looking through a relationship lens impact the role of administrators as supporters of inclusive practices in their schools and communities? In order to successfully carry out the hard work of enacting inclusion, teachers need to know that they are not alone. According to Mogharreban and Bruns (2009), for inclusion to be successful, administrators should be included in discussions about the issues from the start, so that they can provide support and resources as needs arise.

Administrators and supervisors who look through a relationship lens will be able to provide support that goes beyond enforcing the regulations as they make decisions about everyday logistics, assign children and team members to classrooms, and follow through with curricular mandates. Supportive administrators serve as program anchors, providing safe and nurturing spaces for teachers to share ideas, discuss possibilities, and collaboratively problem solve around challenges. Creating an atmosphere of inquiry in which critical discussion is valued and supporting opportunities for teachers and team members to get to know and respect one another as people and not just as professionals, can lay the foundation for more meaningful collaborative efforts to enact inclusive practices (Purcell et al., 2007).

Changing professional dispositions toward inclusion will take time, and must happen within particular classroom, school, and community contexts. Individual teachers who embrace the kinds of changes that are put forth in this book can work toward them more effectively with the support of administrators who are able to act as ambassadors for change in their school communities. Just as we discussed the importance of teacher competencies, administrators must also embody the competencies needed to reframe their own leadership practices. The ways in which they work to set goals for their schools, to give feedback to teachers, and to build relationships with community stakeholders can be instrumental in building the foundation for powerful and meaningful inclusion policies and practices.

As Ainscow (2007) so aptly states,

> becoming more inclusive is a matter of thinking and talking, reviewing and refining practice, and making attempts to develop a more inclusive culture. . . . We cannot divorce inclusion from the contexts within which it is developing, nor the social relationships that might sustain or limit that development. (p. 5)

Administrators who are able to develop supportive relationships with staff and parents that serve as a vehicle for effecting change provide the kind of support that comes not only by way of words but also through taking action (Friend & Shamberger, 2008). Just as we ask teachers to believe that children can be successful, administrators too must believe in the possibility of successful inclusion and demonstrate this belief in the decisions they make each day. Administrators who "walk the talk" can make a lasting and sustainable impact on the future of inclusion for teachers, children, and families.

WHERE DO WE GO FROM FROM HERE? IMPLICATIONS FOR TEACHER PREPARATION AND PROFESSIONAL DEVELOPMENT

Our vision for the future of inclusive early childhood education extends to the higher education settings where early childhood teachers are prepared. As more young children identified with special needs are served in inclusive early childhood programs, it is essential that teacher preparation programs take action to prepare all their students to work with diverse learners. Although inclusion policies have been in place for many years, there remains a gap in teacher preparation such that far too many new teachers still feel unprepared to address the needs of children with disabilities (Couse & Recchia, 2011).

Teacher educators are uniquely situated to inspire their students to take action as advocates for children by helping them to translate the theories and ideals of early childhood inclusion into meaningful practices in the field (Puig & Recchia, 2012). In order to bring the components and competencies to life in their preparation of new teachers, however, teacher educators must first look deeply at their own beliefs and teaching practices, examining their assumptions and biases in light of these ideas.

Reflection, critical inquiry, and supportive mentoring are essential elements of teacher preparation programs that aim to move inclusive practices forward. First, teacher educators need to ask themselves questions such as the following: How am I representing young children with disabilities in my courses? Am I inadvertently presenting a deficit orientation in teaching my students about ways to address special needs? How can I do a better job of making sure that my students are learning to consider the components and competencies as they make decisions about practice? Am I careful to present issues that may arise in practice as opportunities to rethink assumptions and biases? Am I teaching my students to think critically about taken-for-granted practices and policies that they encounter in early childhood classrooms, and to look carefully at their impact on individual children and families?

Early childhood professional preparation programs are also positioned to enact the kinds of relationship-based practices that we've described in this book, modeling for their adult students ways of creating safe and caring learning spaces. How early childhood teacher educators collaborate with each other and with their students can set the tone for building a community of learners within their programs, and can serve as a model from which new teachers will learn to negotiate relationships in their future classrooms and schools. Teacher educators can also help preservice teachers navigate the discrepancies they may be seeing between the early childhood theories they are learning in their courses and some of the practices they are observing in the field, which often play a more powerful role in shaping new teachers' classroom strategies (Recchia et al., 2009).

When faced with real classroom dilemmas, preservice teachers can become discouraged by the barriers to enacting ideal practice that they encounter in the field. Teacher educators are poised to capitalize on these real-life scenarios as opportunities for teaching and learning. Encouraging preservice teachers to consider the kinds of small changes discussed in this book in the moments of their everyday practice, can help them begin to find ways to negotiate presumed barriers to truly make a difference for children. At the same time, teacher educators can use these opportunities to engage their students in thinking about the larger philosophical ideas within which everyday practices are embedded. Providing shared experiences to think deeply about the far-reaching implications of enacting the philosophical ideals of inclusion can have a critical influence on the ways that preservice teachers formulate their own philosophies of teaching and define their roles as educators. In the big picture, quality inclusive teaching is less about exactly what to do in any given moment, and more about the meaning and impact of what is done. As new teachers are learning how to teach inclusively, they will have to address issues within the day-to-day context, while also holding in mind the broader philosophical framework that guides their teaching practice.

In conceptualizing this book, and in our own teaching with preservice teachers, we have approached these ideas with intentionality, as shown in the teaching suggestions presented in the previous chapters. We see everyday challenges to inclusive teaching as catalysts for moving beyond the points of frustration they engender, to find clearer visions for more meaningful practice. Incorporating this approach in early childhood teacher education can help new teachers better see and understand the connections between the small changes they make in everyday practice and the big ideas that guide a reconceptualization of inclusive practice in the field.

In addition to making changes to preservice teacher education, there is also a great need for professional development for in-service teachers who are currently working in early childhood inclusive classrooms. Ongoing professional development that reflects the same principles described above—reflection, critical inquiry, and supportive mentoring—can help guide the process of changing professionals' thinking in ways that will lead to changes in their actions in classrooms and schools. Opportunities to reconceptualize inclusive practices can also be made available to administrators who currently hold leadership roles in inclusive schools or aspire to do so in the future.

As we have reiterated throughout this book, enacting truly inclusive practice is an evolving and dynamic process, which requires continuing development and refining of new skills. Professionals who are committed to rethinking inclusion will benefit from ongoing professional development, as they will never know all they need to know. Ways of thinking and rethinking about teaching and learning will change within each new context and with different teachers and learners. Changes in action don't happen all at once; they take time, thoughtful analysis, negotiation, and support from others.

Our strong belief in the power of early childhood teachers to become advocates for young children with special needs has fueled our passion as early childhood teacher educators. Ultimately, how inclusion is enacted in practice will depend on the quality and effectiveness of the teachers and caregivers who interact directly with young children in inclusive classrooms every day (Buysse & Hollingsworth, 2009; National Professional Development Center on Inclusion, 2009). We believe that even small changes in everyday practice can build momentum toward lasting and significant changes to the field. This "bottom up" perspective (Williams, 1996) on change starts not with a sweeping new policy that is thrust upon teachers from the powers that be, but with a group of committed and caring professionals who are willing to take risks, think "outside the box," and take action to make a difference.

Changing dispositions is hard emotional work that does not happen easily or quickly. We hope that the ideas presented here will help teachers think deeply, and perhaps in new ways, about early childhood inclusion, that will move them one step forward to taking action that will truly make a difference in children's and families' lives.

References

Adair, J. K. (2011, April). *Developing flexibility in young children and early childhood scholars: Ideas from an urban preschool teacher in Bangalore, India.* Paper presented at the annual meeting of the American Education Research Association, New Orleans.

Ainscow, M. (2007). Taking an inclusive turn. *Journal of Research in Special Educational Needs, 7*(1), 3–7.

Baglieri, S., & Knopf, J. H. (2004). Normalizing difference in inclusive teaching. *Journal of Learning Disabilities, 37*(6), 525–529.

Batchelor, D., & Taylor, H. (2005). Social inclusion—the next step: User-friendly strategies to promote social interaction and peer acceptance of children with disabilities. *Australian Journal of Early Childhood, 30*(4), 10–18.

Bergen, D. (2009). Play as the learning medium for future scientists, mathematicians, and engineers. *American Journal of Play, 1*(4), 413–428.

Berry, R. A. W. (2006). Inclusion, power, and community: Teachers and students interpret the language of community in an inclusion classroom. *American Educational Research Journal, 43*(3), 489–529.

Bodrova, E. (2008). Make-believe play versus academic skills: A Vygotskian approach to today's dilemma of early childhood education. *European Early Childhood Education Research Journal, 16*(3), 357–369.

Boyd, B. A., Conroy, M. A., Asmus, J. M., McKenney, E. L. W., & Mancil, G. R. (2008). Descriptive analysis of classroom setting events on the social behaviors of children with autism spectrum disorder. *Education and Training in Developmental Disabilities, 43*(2), 186–197.

Brown, M., & Bergen, D. (2002). Play and social interaction of children with disabilities. *Journal of Research in Childhood Education, 17*(1), 26–37.

Brown, W. H., & Conroy, M. A. (2011). Social-emotional competence in young children with developmental delays: Our reflection and vision for the future. *Journal of Early Intervention, 33*(4), 310–320.

Brown, W. H., Odom, S. L., & McConnell, S. R. (2008). *Social competence of young children: Risk, disability, and evidence-based practices* (2nd ed.). Baltimore: Brookes.

Buysse, V., Goldman, B. D., & Skinner, M. L. (2002). Setting effects on friendship formation among young children with and without disabilities. *Exceptional Children, 68*(4), 503–517.

Buysse, V., & Hollingsworth, H. L. (2009). Program quality and early childhood inclusion: recommendations for professional development. *Topics in Early Childhood Special Education, 29*(2), 119–128.

Carroll, D. (2005). Developing dispositions for teaching: Teacher education programs as moral communities of practice. *The New Educator, 1,* 81–100.

Connor, D. J. (2011). Questioning "normal": Seeing children first and labels second. *National Council of Teachers of English, 16*(2), 1–3.

Couse, L. J., & Recchia, S. L. (2011). From the guest editors: Inclusive early childhood teacher education. *Journal of Early Childhood Teacher Education, 32*(4), 299–301.

Cranton, P. (2006). *Understanding and promoting transformative learning: A guide for educators of adults* (2nd ed.). San Francisco: Jossey-Bass.

Cross, L., Salazar, M. J., Dopson-Campuzano, N., & Batchelder, H. W. (2009). Best practices and considerations: Including young children with disabilities in early childhood settings. *Focus on Exceptional Children, 41*(8), 1–8.

Danforth, S. (2006). From epistemology to democracy: Pragmatism and the reorientation of disability research. *Remedial and Special Education, 27*(6), 337–345.

Danforth, S., & Gabel, S. (Eds.). (2006). *Vital questions facing disability studies in education.* New York: Peter Lang.

DEC/NAEYC (Division for Early Childhood of the Council for Exceptional Children/National Association for the Education of Young Children). (2009). *Early childhood inclusion: A summary.* Chapel Hill: University of North Carolina, Frank Porter Graham Child Development Institute.

Dewey, J. (1998). What is thinking? In *How we think* (pp. 3–16). Boston: Houghton Mifflin. (Original work published 1933)

Dunlap, G., & Fox, L. (2011). Function-based interventions for children with challenging behavior. *Journal of Early Intervention, 33*(4), 333–343.

Elliot, E. (2010). Thinking beyond a framework: Entering into dialogues. In V. Pacini-Ketchabaw (Ed.), *Flows, rhythms, and intensities of early childhood education curriculum* (pp. 3–20). New York: Peter Lang.

Erwin, E., & Guintini, M. (2000). Inclusion and classroom membership in early childhood. *International Journal of Disability, Development and Education, 47*(3), 237–257.

Estell, D. B., Jones, M. H., Pearl, R., & Van Acker, R. V. (2009). Best friendships of students with and without learning disabilities across late elementary school. *Exceptional Children, 76*(1), 110–124.

Estell, D. B., Jones, M. H., Pearl, R., Van Acker, R. V., Farmer, T. W., & Rodkin, P. C. (2008). Peer groups, popularity, and social preference: Trajectories of social functioning among students with and without learning disabilities. *Journal of Learning Disabilities, 41,* 5–14.

Friedlander, D. (2009). Sam comes to school: Including students with autism in your classroom. *Clearing House, 82*(3), 141–144.

Friend, M., & Shamberger, C. (2008). Inclusion. In T. Good (Ed.), *21st century education: A reference handbook* (pp. II-124–II-130). Thousand Oaks, CA: Sage.

Gabel, S. L. (2005). Introduction: Disability studies in education. In S. L. Gabel (Ed.), *Disability studies in education: Readings in theory and method* (pp. 1–20). New York: Peter Lang.

Gilliam, W. S., & Shahar, G. (2006). Preschool and child care expulsion and suspension: Rates and predictors in one state. *Infants & Young Children, 19*(3), 228–245.

Gordon, P. A., Feldman, A., & Chiriboga, J. M. (2005). Helping children with disabilities develop and maintain friendships. *Teacher Education and Special Education, 28*(1), 1–9.

Grisham-Brown, J., Hemmeter, M. L., & Pretti-Frontczak, K. (2005). *Blended practices for teaching young children in inclusive settings.* Baltimore: Brookes.

Guralnick, M. J. (2001). *Early childhood inclusion: Focus on change.* Baltimore: Brookes.

Guralnick, M. J. (2006). Peer relationships and the mental health of young children with intellectual delays. *Journal of Policy and Practice in Intellectual Disabilities, 3*(1), 49–56.

Guralnick, M. J. (2010). Early intervention approaches to enhance the peer-related social competence of young children with developmental delays: A historical perspective. *Infants & Young Children, 23*, 73–83.

Guralnick, M. J., Connor, R. T., Hammond, M. A., Gottman, J. M., & Kinnish, K. (1996). The peer relations of preschool children with communication disorders. *Child Development, 67*, 471–489.

Guralnick, M. J., Connor, R. T., & Johnson, L. C. (2011). Peer-related social competence of young children with Down syndrome. *American Journal on Intellectual and Developmental Disabilities, 116*, 48–64.

Guralnick, M. J., Hammond, M. A., & Connor, R. T. (2006). Nonsocial play patterns of young children with communication disorders: Implications for behavioral adaptation. *Early Education and Development, 7*(2), 203–228.

Guralnick, M. J., Neville, B., Hammond, M. A., & Connor, R. T. (2007). The friendships of young children with developmental delays: A longitudinal analysis. *Journal of Applied Developmental Psychology, 28*, 64–79.

Hamilton, D. (2005). An eco-behavioural analysis of interactive engagement of children with developmental disabilities with their peers in inclusive preschools. *International Journal of Disability, Development and Education, 52*(2), 121–137.

Hamre, B. K., Pianta, R. C., Burchinal, M., Field, S., LoCasale-Crouch, J., Downer, J. T., . . . Scott-Little, C. (2012). A course on effective teacher-child interactions: Effects on teacher beliefs, knowledge, and observed practice. *American Educational Research Journal, 49*(1), 88–123.

Harper, L. V., & McCluskey, K. S. (2002). Caregiver and peer response to children with language and motor disabilities in inclusive preschool programs. *Early Childhood Research Quarterly, 17*, 148–166.

Heffron, M. C., Ivins, B., & Weston, D. R. (2005). Finding an authentic voice—Use of self: Essential learning processes for relationship-based work. *Infants and Young Children, 18*(4), 323–336.

Hehir, T. (2005). *New directions in special education: Eliminating ableism in policy and practice.* Cambridge, MA: Harvard Education Press.

Hestenes, L. L., & Carroll, D. E. (2000). The play interactions of young children with and without disabilities: Individual and environmental influences. *Early Childhood Research Quarterly, 15*(2), 229–246.

Horn, E. M., Thompson, B., Palmer, S., Jenson, R., & Turbiville, V. (2004). Preschool. In C. H. Kennedy & E. M. Horn (Eds.), *Including students with severe disabilities* (pp. 207–221). Boston: Pearson/Allyn & Bacon.

Howes, C., & Hamilton, C. E. (1992). Children's relationships with caregivers: Mothers and child care teachers. *Child Development, 63,* 859–878.

Howes, C., & Ritchie, S. (2002). *A matter of trust: Connecting teachers and learners in the early childhood classroom.* New York: Teachers College Press.

Hyatt, K. J. (2007). The new IDEA: Changes, concerns, and questions. *Intervention in School and Clinic, 42,* 131–136.

Kagan, D. M. (1992). Professional growth among preservice and beginning teachers. *Review of Educational Research, 62*(2), 129–169.

Kaufman, D. (1996). Constructivist-based experiential learning in teacher education. *Action in Teacher Education, 18,* 40–50.

Kemple, K. M. (2004). *Let's be friends: Peer competence and social inclusion in early childhood programs.* New York: Teachers College Press.

Kliewer, C. (2006). Disability studies and young children. In S. Danforth & S. Gabel (Eds.), *Vital questions facing disability studies in education* (pp. 91–102). New York: Peter Lang.

Kliewer, C. (2008). *Seeing all kids as readers: A new vision for literacy in the inclusive early childhood classroom.* Baltimore: Brookes.

Kliewer, C., & Biklen, D. (2007). Enacting literacy: Local understanding, significant disability, and a new frame for educational opportunity. *Teachers College Record, 109*(12), 2579–2600.

Kliewer, C., Fitzgerald, L. M., Meyer-Mork, J., Hartman, P., English-Sand, P., & Raschke, D. (2004). Citizenship for all in the literate community: An ethnography of young children with significant disabilities in inclusive early childhood settings. *Harvard Educational Review, 74*(4), 373–402.

Kluth, P., & Schwartz, P. (2008). *"Just give him the whale": Ways to use fascinations, areas of expertise, and strengths to support students with autism.* Baltimore: Brookes.

Kopp, C. B., Baker, B. L., & Brown, K. W. (1992). Social skills and their correlates: Preschoolers with developmental delays. *American Journal on Mental Retardation, 96*(4), 357–366.

Kostelnik, M., Onaga, E., Rohde, B., & Whiren, A. (2001). *Children with special needs: Lessons for early childhood professionals.* New York: Teachers College Press.

Lee, S., Yoo, S., & Bak, S. (2003). Characteristics of friendships between children with and without mild disabilities. *Education and Training in Developmental Disabilities, 38,* 157–166.

Lee, Y.-J., & Recchia, S. L. (2008). Who's the boss? Young children's power and influence in an early childhood classroom. *Early Childhood Research and Practice, 10*(1). Retrieved from http://ecrp.uiuc.edu/v10n1/lee.html

Lortie, D. (1975). *School teacher: A sociological study.* Chicago: University of Chicago Press.

Lubeck, S. (1991). Reconceptualizing early childhood education: A response. *Early Education and Development, 2*(2), 168–174.

Martin, J. K., Pescosolido, B. A., & Tuch, S. A. (2000). Of fear and loathing: The role of "disturbing behaviors," labels, and causal attributions in shaping public attitudes toward people with mental illness. *Journal of Health and Social Behavior, 41*, 208–223.

Mezirow, J. (1997). Transformative learning: Theory to practice. *New Directions for Adult and Continuing Education, 74*, 5–12.

Mogharreban, C. C., & Bruns, D. A. (2009). Moving to inclusive pre-kindergarten classrooms: Lessons from the field. *Early Childhood Education Journal, 36*, 407–414.

Mullarkey, L. S., Recchia, S. L., Lee, S. Y., Lee, Y.-J., & Shin, M. S. (2005). Manipulative managers and devilish dictators: Teachers' perspectives on the dilemmas and challenges of classroom leadership. *Journal of Early Childhood Teacher Education, 25*, 123–129.

Naraian, S. (2011). Seeking transparency: The production of an inclusive classroom community. *International Journal of Inclusive Education, 15*(9), 955–973.

National Professional Development Center on Inclusion (NPDCI). (2009). *Why program quality matters for early childhood inclusion: Recommendations for professional development.* Chapel Hill: University of North Carolina, Frank Porter Graham Child Development Institute, NPDCI. Retrieved from http://www.tats.ucf.edu/docs/npdci-quality-paper.pdf

Odom, S. L. (2000). Preschool inclusion: What we know and where we go from here. *Topics in Early Childhood Special Education, 20*(1), 20–27.

Odom, S. L., Buysse, V., & Soukakou, E. (2011). Inclusion for young children with disabilities: A quarter century of research perspectives. *Journal of Early Intervention, 33*(4), 344–356.

Odom, S. L., Vitztum, J., Wolery, R., Lieber, J., Sandall, S., Hanson, M. J., . . . Horn, E. (2004). Preschool inclusion in the United States: A review of research from an ecological systems perspective. *Journal of Research in Special Educational Needs, 4*(1), 17–49.

Odom, S. L., Zercher, C., & Li, S. (2006). Social acceptance and rejection of preschool children with disabilities: A mixed-method analysis. *Journal of Educational Psychology, 98*(4), 807–823.

Odom S. L., Zercher, C., Marquart, J., Li, S., Sandall, S. R., & Wolfberg, P. (2002). Social relationships of children with disabilities and their peers in inclusive preschool classrooms. In S. L. Odom (Ed.), *Widening the circle: Including children with disabilities in preschool programs* (pp. 61–80). New York: Teachers College Press.

Pedro, J. (2006). Taking reflection into the real world of teaching. *Kappa Delta Pi, 42*(3),129–132.

Puig, V. I., & Recchia, S. L. (2012). Urban advocates for young children with special needs: First-year early childhood teachers enacting social justice. *The New Educator, 8*(3), 258–277.

Purcell, M. L., Horn, E., & Palmer, S. (2007). A qualitative study of the initiation and continuation of preschool inclusion programs. *Exceptional Children, 74*(1), 85–99.

Recchia, S. L., Beck, L., Esposito, A., & Tarrant, K. (2009). Diverse field experiences as a catalyst for preparing high-quality early childhood teachers. *Journal of Early Childhood Teacher Education, 30*, 105–122.

Recchia, S. L., & Dvorakova, K. (2012). How three young toddlers transition from an infant to a toddler child care classroom: Exploring the influence of peer relationships, teacher expectations, and changing social contexts. *Early Education and Development, 23*(2), 181–201.

Recchia, S. L., & Soucacou, E. P. (2006). Nurturing social experiences in three early childhood special education classrooms. *Early Childhood Research and Practice, 8*(2). Retrieved from http://ecrp.uiuc.edu/v8n2/recchia.html

Richardson, P. K. (2002). The school as social context: Social interaction patterns of children with physical disabilities. *The American Journal of Occupational Therapy, 56*(3), 296–304.

Rodgers, C. (2002). Defining reflection: Another look at John Dewey and reflective thinking. *Teachers College Record, 104*(4), 842–866.

Rogoff, B. (2003). *The cultural nature of human development*. New York: Oxford University Press.

Stanton-Chapman, T. L., & Hadden, D. S. (2011). Encouraging peer interactions in preschool classrooms: The role of the teacher. *Young Exceptional Children, 14*(1), 17–28.

Strain, P. S., & Bovey, E. H., II. (2011). Randomized, controlled trial of the LEAP Model of early intervention for young children with autism spectrum disorders. *Topics in Early Childhood Special Education, 31*(3), 133–154.

Strain, P. S., Schwartz, I. S., & Barton, E. E. (2011). Providing interventions for young children with autism spectrum disorders: What we still need to accomplish. *Journal of Early Intervention, 33*(4), 321–332.

Tomlinson, C. A. (2001). *How to differentiate instruction in mixed-ability classrooms*. Columbus, OH: Merrill Prentice Hall.

U.S. Department of Education. (2004). *Twenty-sixth annual report to Congress on the implementation of the Individuals with Disabilities Education Act*. Washington, DC: U.S. Government Printing Office.

Valle, J. W., & Connor, D. J. (2011). *Rethinking disability: A disability studies approach to inclusive practices*. New York: McGraw Hill.

Walker, D. B., & Berthelsen, D. (2008). Children with autistic spectrum disorder in early childhood education. *International Journal of Early Childhood, 40*(1), 33–51.

Wen, X., Elicker, J. G., & McMullen, M. B. (2011). Early childhood teachers' curriculum beliefs: Are they consistent with observed classroom practices? *Early Education and Development, 22*(6), 945–969.

Wiener, J., & Schneider, B. (2002). A multisource exploration of friendship patterns of children with and without LD. *Journal of Abnormal Child Psychology, 30*, 127–141.

Williams, L. R. (1996). Does theory lead practice? Teachers' constructs about teaching: Bottom up perspectives. In J. A. Chafel & S. Reifel (Eds.), *Theory and practice in early childhood teaching* (pp. 153–184). Greenwich, CT: JAI Press.

Index

Abigail (student), 49–55
  child characteristics, 13, 50–52,
    55
  classroom component 6: support
    of many types for children to
    meet full potential, 9, 13, 39,
    49–55, 56–57
  classroom context, 13, 49–50,
    56–57
  questions for further reflection, 58
  teacher interactions with, 53–55,
    56–57, 67–68, 69
Adair, J. K., 64
Adam (student), 23–28
  child characteristics, 12, 24–26
  classroom component 2:
    opportunities for interpersonal
    connections and social support,
    8, 12, 17–18, 23–28, 33
  classroom context, 12, 23–24
  physical disabilities and
    independence needs, 23–28
  questions for further reflection,
    34–35
  support for independence and
    self-esteem, 26–28, 70, 72–73
  welcoming to classroom, 24–26
Administrative leadership, 90–92
Aggressive and/or violent children,
  44–49
Ainscow, M., 91
Asmus, J. M., 5, 16, 28–29
Aurelia (teacher)
  classroom component 1: multiple
    ways of engaging in teaching
    and learning, 8, 12, 17, 18–23,
    33
  observation of Mario, 21–23, 71
  questions for further reflection,
    34
  teacher characteristics, 12, 21–22
Autism Spectrum Disorder (ASD),
  16, 28

Baglieri, S., 2
Baker, B. L., 4, 15, 16
Barton, E. E., 61
Batchelder, H. W., 88–90
Batchelor, D., 62
Beck, L., 63, 93
Behavioral control limitation myth
  of inclusion, 61
Bergen, D., 16, 71
Berry, R. A. W., 3, 38
Berthelsen, D., 5, 15, 28
Beverly (teacher)
  classroom component 4:
    individual differences integrated
    into curriculum, 8, 13, 38–39,
    40–44, 56, 57
  questions for further reflection,
    57
  teacher characteristics, 13, 42–43,
    56, 69–70, 75
Biklen, D., 6–7, 68, 69
Bodrova, E., 71
Bovey, E. H., II, 16
Boyd, B. A., 5, 16, 28–29
Brown, K. W., 4, 15, 16
Brown, M., 16
Brown, W. H., 15, 62–63
Bruns, D. A., 14, 87, 89, 91
Burchinal, M., 61, 63, 66
Buysse, V., 4, 5–6, 16, 37, 60, 94

Camille (teacher)
    classroom component 5: all
        students as integral members of
        classroom community, 8, 13, 39,
        44–49, 56
    questions for further reflection, 58
    teacher characteristics, 13, 45,
        47–49, 55, 56, 74–75, 76, 78
Carroll, D. E., 4–5, 16, 61, 66
Chiriboga, J. M., 37
Classroom components of inclusion,
        8–9, 10–11, 14–58
    applying, 87–92
    community and inclusive
        practice, 84–85
    component 1: multiple ways
        of engaging in teaching and
        learning, 8, 12, 17, 18–23, 33
    component 2: opportunities for
        interpersonal connections and
        social support, 8, 12, 17–18,
        23–28, 33
    component 3: environment
        design for differences, 8, 12, 18,
        28–32, 33–34
    component 4: individual
        differences integrated into
        curriculum, 8, 13, 38–39, 40–44,
        56, 57
    component 5: all students as
        integral members of classroom
        community, 8, 13, 39, 44–49, 56
    component 6: support of many
        types for children to meet full
        potential, 9, 13, 39, 49–55,
        56–57
    synthesizing through relationship
        lens, 83–84, 88
Cody (student), 44–49
    child characteristics, 13, 45–47,
        55
    classroom component 5: all
        students as integral members of
        classroom community, 8, 13, 39,
        44–49, 56
    classroom context, 13, 45, 56

questions for further reflection, 58
teacher support in developing
    social and coping skills, 47–48,
    55, 56, 74–75, 76, 78
Community, inclusion and, 84–85
Connor, D. J., 3, 4, 6, 7, 59, 63, 68,
    72, 74
Connor, R. T., 4, 5, 15, 37
Conroy, M. A., 5, 16, 28–29, 62–63
Couse, L. J., 92
Cranton, P., 64
Cross, L., 88–90
Curriculum
    individual differences integrated
        into, 8, 13, 38–39, 40–44, 56, 57
    to reflect and include all children,
        87–89

Danforth, S., 6, 7, 59, 76, 86
DEC (Division for Early Childhood,
    Council of Exceptional
    Children), 2, 60, 89–90
Developmental delays, 40–44, 61–62
Dewey, J., 63, 64
Disability Studies in Education (DSE)
    philosophy, 6–8, 63, 68, 72, 76,
    86–87
Division for Early Childhood,
    Council of Exceptional Children
    (DEC), 2, 60, 89–90
Dopson-Campuzano, N., 88–90
Downer, J. T., 61, 63, 66
DSE (Disability Studies in Education)
    philosophy, 6–8, 63, 68, 72, 76,
    86–87
Dunlap, G., 74
Dvorakova, K., 39
Dynamic process, inclusion as,
    85–86

Elicker, J. G., 62, 63
Elliot, E., 63
English-Sand, P., 6–7
Erwin, E., 3, 6
Esposito, A., 63, 93
Estell, D. B., 6, 37

Farmer, T. W., 37
Feldman, A., 37
Field, S., 61, 63, 66
Fitzgerald, L. M., 6–7
Fox, L., 74
Friedlander, D., 62
Friend, M., 84, 89, 92

Gabel, S. L., 6, 86, 87
Gandhi, Mohandas, 59
Gilliam, W. S., 39
Goldman, B. D., 4, 5–6, 16, 37
Gordon, P. A., 37
Gottman, J. M., 15
Grisham-Brown, J., 82
Guintini, M., 3, 6
Guralnick, M. J., 4–6, 14, 15, 19, 37,
    61, 62, 65, 82

Hadden, D. S., 68
Hamilton, C. E., 39
Hamilton, D., 16
Hammond, M. A., 4, 5, 15, 37
Hamre, B. K., 61, 63, 66
Hanson, M. J., 2, 5
Harper, L. V., 62
Hartman, P., 6–7
Heffron, M. C., 65
Hehir, T., 59
Hemmeter, M. L., 82
Hestenes, L. L., 4–5, 16, 61
Hollingsworth, H. L., 94
Horn, E. M., 2, 4, 5, 85, 87, 91
Howes, C., 39, 82
Hyatt, K. J., 85
Hydrocephalus, 23–28
Hypotonia, 18–23

Inclusion
    barriers to, 61
    broader research framework on,
        3–4
    building social community in
        early childhood classrooms, 2,
        82–94
    challenges for teachers, 60–61
    challenges of high-quality
        teaching for, 2–3
    challenge to dominant discourse
        on, 6–8
    of children with challenging
        behaviors, 36–39
    classroom components of, 8–9,
        14–58
    deficit-focused approach and, 6
    defined, 3
    diversity as norm, 2, 59, 79
    for empowering all students,
        36–58
    "inclusion myths," 61
    long-term social interactions and,
        5–6
    many faces of, 1–3
    meanings of, 3
    "normative" social development
        and, 6
    peer culture in classroom and. See
        Peer culture
    power relationships and, 37–38,
        40, 41–44
    principles of inclusive practice,
        84–87
    of students with special needs,
        14–35
    teacher competencies for, 9, 11,
        59–81
    traditional approach to, 4–6
    visions for future, 82–94
Ira (student), 40–44
    child characteristics, 13, 41, 55,
        69–70, 75
    classroom component 4:
        individual differences integrated
        into curriculum, 8, 13, 38–39,
        40–44, 56, 57
    classroom context, 13, 40, 41–44,
        56, 57
    questions for further reflection, 57
Ivins, B., 65

Jenny (teacher)
    classroom component 2:

Jenny (teacher), *continued*
    opportunities for interpersonal
      connections and social support,
      8, 12, 17–18, 23–28, 33
    questions for further reflection,
      34–35
    support for independence of
      Adam, 26–28, 70–71, 72–73
    teacher characteristics, 12, 26–28
Jenson, R., 85
Joey (student), 28–32
    child characteristics, 12, 28–30
    classroom component 3:
      environment design for
      differences, 8, 12, 18, 28–32,
      33–34
    classroom context, 12, 29–30
    questions for further reflection, 35
    teacher responses to, 30–32, 68,
      73, 76–77
    welcoming to classroom, 29–30
Johnson, L. C., 4, 5
Jones, M. H., 6, 37

Kagan, D. M., 63, 64
Kathy (teacher)
    classroom component 3:
      environment design for
      differences, 8, 12, 18, 28–32,
      33–34
    questions for further reflection, 35
    responses to Joey, 30–32, 68, 73,
      76–77
    teacher characteristics, 12, 30–32,
      68
Kaufman, D., 64
Kemple, K. M., 49, 60–62, 66
Kinnish, K., 15
Kliewer, C., 3, 6–7, 68, 69
Kluth, P., 77
Knopf, J. H., 2
Kopp, C. B., 4, 15, 16
Kostelnik, M., 4

Lee, S. Y., 77
Lee, Y.-J., 38, 40, 65, 77

Li, S., 16, 37, 40
Lieber, J., 2, 5
LoCasale-Crouch, J., 61, 63, 66
Lorna (teacher)
    classroom component 6: support
      of many types for children to
      meet full potential, 9, 13, 39,
      49–55, 56–57
    questions for further reflection, 58
    teacher characteristics, 13, 49–50,
      52–53, 67–68, 69
Lortie, D., 64
Lubeck, S., 63

Mancil, G. R., 5, 16, 28–29
Mario (student), 18–23
    child characteristics, 12, 20
    classroom component 1: multiple
      ways of engaging in teaching
      and learning, 8, 12, 17, 18–23,
      33
    classroom context, 12, 19
    inclusion within mixed-age
      group, 19
    interaction with Jane in sandbox,
      22–23, 71
    observation by teacher, 21–23
    questions for further reflection, 34
    welcoming to classroom, 20
Marquart, J., 37, 40
Martin, J. K., 37
Mary (teacher)
    classroom component 6: support
      of many types for children to
      meet full potential, 9, 13, 39,
      49–55, 56–57
    questions for further reflection, 58
    teacher characteristics, 13, 49–50,
      52–55, 67–68, 69
McCluskey, K. S., 62
McConnell, S. R., 15
McKenney, E. L. W., 5, 16, 28–29
McMullen, M. B., 62, 63
Meyer-Mork, J., 6–7
Mezirow, J., 64
Mogharreban, C. C., 14, 87, 89, 91

Mullarkey, L. S., 77

NAEYC (National Association for the
    Education of Young Children),
    2, 60
Naraian, S., 87
National Association for the
    Education of Young Children
    (NAEYC), 2, 60
National Professional Development
    Center on Inclusion (NPDCI), 94
Neville, B., 4, 15, 37

Odom, S. L., 2, 5, 15, 16, 37, 40, 60
Onaga, E., 4
Overstimulation myth of inclusion,
    61

Palmer, S., 4, 85, 87, 91
Pearl, R., 6, 37
Pedro, J., 63, 64
Peer culture, 37–38
    power relationships in, 37–38, 40,
        41–44
    rejection and, 37, 40, 41–44
Pervasive Developmental Disorders
    (PDD), 28–32
Pescosolido, B. A., 37
Pianta, R. C., 61, 63, 66
Power relationships, in peer culture,
    37–38, 40, 41–44
Pretti-Frontczak, K., 82
Principles of inclusive practice,
    84–87
    principle 1: inclusion is about
        community, 84–85
    principle 2: inclusion as dynamic
        process, 85–86
    principle 3: inclusion is about
        social transformation, 86–87
Professional development of
    teachers, 62–63, 92–94
Puig, V. I., 92
Purcell, M. L., 4, 87, 91

Quality of life issues in inclusion, 61

Raschke, D., 6–7
Reah (teacher)
    classroom component 4:
        individual differences integrated
        into curriculum, 8, 13, 38–39,
        40–44, 56, 57
    questions for further reflection, 57
    teacher characteristics, 13, 42–43,
        56, 69–70
Recchia, S. L., 38, 39, 40, 61, 62, 63,
    65, 77, 92, 93
Rejection, 37, 40, 41–44
Richardson, P. K., 24
Ritchie, S., 82
Rodgers, C., 63–65
Rodkin, P. C., 37
Rogoff, B., 81
Rohde, B., 4

Salazar, M. J., 88–90
Sandall, S. R., 2, 5, 37, 40
Schneider, B., 37
Schwartz, I. S., 61
Schwartz, P., 77
Scott-Little, C., 61, 63, 66
Self-awareness, of teacher, 70
Self-Contained Preschool Special
    Education Classroom, 24
Shahar, G., 39
Shamberger, C., 84, 89, 92
Shin, M. S., 77
Shy children, 49–55
Skinner, M. L., 4, 5–6, 16, 37
Social inclusion. See Inclusion
Social transformation role of
    inclusion, 86–87
Soucacou, E. P., 60–62, 77
Special Education Itinerant Teacher
    (SEIT), 41
Spina bifida, 23–28
Stanton-Chapman, T. L., 68
Strain, P. S., 16, 61
Student characteristics. See also
    names of specific students
    overview of, 12–13
    positive responses to diverse

Student characteristics, *continued*
  abilities, 17–18
  social competencies of young
    children with special needs,
    15–16

Tarrant, K., 63, 93
Taylor, H., 62
Teacher competencies for inclusion
    in classroom, 9, 11, 59–81. *See
    also names of specific teachers*
  administrative leadership to
    support, 90–92
  applying, 80, 87–92
  bridging developmental
    differences, 32–34
  challenges of inclusion, 60–61
  collaboration with professionals
    and families, 89–90
  competency 1: ways of thinking/
    ways of being to embrace
    difference and capitalize on
    opportunities, 9, 67–69, 80
  competency 2: capacity to nurture
    and embrace child as unique
    individual, 9, 69–70, 80
  competency 3: openness to
    reconsidering, rethinking,
    redoing teaching and learning
    activities, 9, 70–72, 80
  competency 4: ability to attend to
    child's perspective, 9, 72–74, 80
  competency 5: expectation
    that all children can meet
    educational/developmental
    goals, 9, 74–76, 80
  competency 6: understanding of
    "equity" versus "equality," 9,
    76–78, 80
  facilitating social interactions
    in early childhood classrooms,
    61–63
  as framework for transforming
    teaching and learning in early
    childhood, 78–81
  implications for teacher

  preparation and professional
    development, 92–94
  inclusion as dynamic process,
    85–86
  inclusive curriculum, 87–89
  professional development for,
    62–63, 92–94
  reconceptualization of early
    childhood inclusive teaching,
    63–65
  synthesizing through relationship
    lens, 83–84, 88
Teacher preparation, 92–94
Thompson, B., 85
Tomlinson, C. A., 88
Tuch, S. A., 37
Turbiville, V., 85
Tutorial instruction myth of
    inclusion, 61

U.S. Department of Education, 3

Valle, J. W., 3, 4, 6, 7, 59, 63, 68, 72,
    74
Van Acker, R. V., 6, 37
Vitztum, J., 2, 5

Walker, D. B., 5, 15, 28
Wen, X., 62, 63
Weston, D. R., 65
Whiren, A., 4
Wiener, J., 37
Williams, L. R., 64, 94
Wolery, R., 2, 5
Wolfberg, P., 37, 40

Zercher, C., 16, 37, 40

About the Authors

Susan L. Recchia, PhD, is associate professor and coordinator of the Program in Early Childhood Special Education at Teachers College, Columbia University. She serves as faculty director of the Rita Gold Early Childhood Center, an inclusive and culturally responsive center for early education, professional preparation, research, and outreach. Professor Recchia brings an extensive background in early development and years of practice in early intervention to her current position, where she teaches and supervises master's degree and doctoral students who are studying early childhood education and early childhood special education. Her research interests include the role of social and emotional experiences in early learning, inclusive early care and education, and early childhood teacher development.

Yoon-Joo Lee, EdD, is an assistant professor in the Department of Childhood, Bilingual, and Special Education in the School of Education at Brooklyn College, City University of New York. She teaches and supervises master's degree students in the Graduate Program in Early Childhood Special Education. Dr. Lee had several years of experience in teaching infants, toddlers, and preschoolers in different early childhood special education classrooms before joining the faculty at Brooklyn College. Her scholarly interests include social experiences of young children with special needs in early childhood classrooms and the experiences of families of children with special needs from culturally and linguistically diverse backgrounds.